D1124752

Paris

0 — 1 km

0 — 1 mile

CONTENTS

ABOUT THIS BOOK

This *Step by Step Guide* has been produced by the editors of Insight Guides, whose books have set the standard for visual travel guides since 1970. With top-quality photography and authoritative recommendations, this guidebook brings you the very best of the French capital in a series of 20 tailor-made tours.

WALKS AND TOURS

The tours in the book provide something to suit all budgets, tastes and trip lengths. As well as covering Paris's classic attractions, of which there are myriad, the routes track lesser-known sights and up-and-coming areas; there are also excursions for those who want to extend their visit outside the capital.

The tours embrace a range of interests, so whether you are an art enthusiast, an architecture buff, a gourmet, a lover of flora and fauna, a historian or royalist, or have children to entertain, you will find an option to suit.

We recommend that you read the whole of a tour before setting out. This should help you to familiarise yourself with the route and enable you to plan where to

Above from top: ornamental lamps at Versailles; at the Palais de Tokyo, which is home to two museums; stone sculpture outside St-Eustache church; service with a smile in smart uniforms; boating in the sunshine at Versailles.

stop for refreshments – options for this are shown in the 'Food and Drink' boxes, recognisable by the knife and fork sign.

For our pick of the walks by theme, consult Recommended Tours For… *(see pp.6–7).*

OVERVIEW

The tours are set in context by this introductory section, giving an overview of the city to set the scene, plus background information on food and drink and shopping. A succinct history timeline in this chapter highlights the key events that have shaped Paris over the centuries.

DIRECTORY

Also supporting the tours is a Directory chapter, comprising a user-friendly, clearly organised A-Z of practical information, our pick of where to stay while you are in the city and select restaurant listings; these eateries complement the more low-key cafés and restaurants that feature within the tours themselves and are intended to offer a wider choice for evening dining. Nightlife listings are also included here.

The Author

Arts and travel writer Michael Macaroon has spent a considerable amount of time in France over the years, especially in Paris, where he studied at the Sorbonne. He has a particular interest in French art and food and is a regular contributor to a number of journals on those subjects. His fascination with France is partly owing to the ability of the French to do so many things so well: art and architecture, food and wine, cinema and theatre, style and fashion. He is also the author of Insight's *Paris Smart Guide*.

Margin Tips
Shopping tips, quirky anecdotes, historical facts and interesting snippets help visitors to make the most of their time in Paris.

Feature Boxes
Notable topics are highlighted in these special boxes.

Key Facts Box
This box gives details of the distance covered on the tour, plus an estimate of how long it should take. It also states where the route starts and finishes, and gives key travel information such as which days are best to do the tour or handy transport tips.

Route Map
Detailed cartography with the walk or tour clearly plotted using numbered dots. For more detailed mapping, see the pull-out map, which is slotted inside the back cover.

Food and Drink
Recommendations of where to stop for refreshment are given in these boxes. The numbers prior to each café/ restaurant name link to references in the main text. Places recommended en route are also plotted on the maps.

The € signs given in each entry reflect the approximate cost of a two-course meal for one, with half a bottle of house wine. These should be seen as a guide only. Price ranges, which are also quoted on the inside back flap for easy reference, are as follows:

€€€€ €75 and above
€€€ €50–75
€€ €30–50
€ €30 and below

Footers
Look here for the tour name, a map reference and the main attraction on the double-page.

SHOPPERS

The department stores on the Grands Boulevards (walk 4), the boutiques of the Marais and Bastille (walk 6) and the bookshops of the Latin Quarter (walk 7).

RECOMMENDED TOURS FOR...

CLASSIC CAFÉS

Take it easy with the bohemian crowd in the Marais (walk 6) or sip coffee like the existentialists at the Deux Magots and the Café de Flore in St-Germain (walk 8).

ESCAPING THE CROWDS

Find a quiet corner at Père-Lachaise cemetery (walk 11) or head off the beaten tourist track to the up-and-coming northeast (tour 12) or the smart 16th *arrondissement* (walk 14).

CHILDREN

Try boating in the Tuileries or Jardin du Luxembourg (walks 2 and 8), combine the zoo and the dinosaurs at the Jardin des Plantes (walk 7) or head out of the capital to Disneyland (tour 20).

PARKS AND GARDENS

Take a break in main parks such as the Tuileries and the Luxembourg (walks 2 and 8), or sample less well-known green spaces including the impressively planned Parc des Buttes-Chaumont (walk 12).

FOOD AND WINE

The 7th (walk 3), home to some of the city's best restaurants, the Champs-Élysées (walk 4) for Ladurée macaroons, rue Mouffetard (walk 7), with its vibrant food market, Bercy (walk 13), site of the city's former wine warehouses, or Passy (walk 14) for its wine museum.

ART ENTHUSIASTS

From the big three – the Louvre (walk 2), Musée d'Orsay (walk 3) and Centre Pompidou (walk 5) – to more intimate showcases such as the Musée Rodin (walk 3), the exquisite Musée Jacquemart-André (walk 4) or Monet's house out at Giverny (tour 19).

LITERARY TYPES

Pay homage to Victor Hugo in the Marais (walk 6), rifle through racks of antiquarian books in the Latin Quarter (walk 7) or visit Balzac's house in Passy (walk 14).

ROMANTIC PARIS

Take a stroll along the Seine by the pretty Île St-Louis (walk 1) or enjoy an early morning walk up the steps of the Sacré-Coeur (walk 9).

ROYALISTS

Follow in the steps of kings and emperors, whether Louis IX at Sainte-Chapelle (walk 1), Philippe-Auguste at the Louvre (walk 2), Napoleon at Malmaison (tour 16) and Fontainebleau (tour 18) or Louis XIV at Versailles (tour 17).

OVERVIEW

An overview of the geography, customs, culture and architecture in Paris, plus illuminating background information on food and drink, shopping and history.

CITY INTRODUCTION

With two World Heritage sites, 136 museums, over 450 parks and gardens, and 171 churches and temples, it's not surprising that the population of 2.2 million have to share their good fortune with around 30 million visitors a year.

Revolutionaries
Uprisings, protests, revolutions, strikes, marches: the Parisians seem to love them all. In 2003 there were so many marches and strikes that there was eventually even a major protest march against strikes themselves.

Paris is a comparatively compact city and more suited to walking than many, particularly for a capital. The city runs for 13km (8 miles) east and west, around 9km (6 miles) north and south, and is contained by the Périphérique, a famously traffic-logged ring road that runs 35km (22 miles) around it. The suburbs *(la banlieue)* form two concentric rings around Paris, and are split into *départements* or counties.

Family Values

As part of the government's policy to encourage population growth in France, each *famille nombreuse* (ie with three children or more) is rewarded with benefits including nursery provision, subsidised public transport, sports equipment, car tax and school meals, and free admission to museums. The birth rate, which the National Institute for Statistics now measures at more than two births per woman, has been boosted by France's large Muslim community, which could become a majority in the next 20 to 25 years, if demographic trends continue.

RIVER SEINE

The city is cut through the middle by the River Seine, which is spanned by 37 bridges. The river is the city's calmest – and widest – artery, barely ruffled by the daily flow of tourist and commercial boat traffic. It enters Paris close to the Bois de Vincennes in the southeast and meanders gently north and south past three small islands: Île St-Louis, Île de la Cité and, on its way out, Île des Cygnes.

Chains of hillocks rise up to the north of the river, including Montmartre (the highest point of the city), Ménilmontant, Belleville and Buttes-Chaumont (*butte* means 'hill'); and, to the south, Montsouris, the Mont Ste-Geneviève, Buttes aux Cailles and Maison Blanche.

CITY LAYOUT

One of the most persistent images of Paris is of elegant long avenues lined with huge chestnut and plane trees. Chains of broad boulevards encircle the centre of the city, marking where the boundary was in medieval times. Many of the capital's streets contain the word *faubourg*, indicating that they were once part of the suburb outside the city wall.

Arrondissements

In fact, the capital is organised into *arrondissements* (districts), which spiral outwards in a neat snail-shell pattern from the Île-de-France (the 1st *arrondissement*) to the northeast (the 20th). All of these are contained within the Périphérique ring road. When Parisians explain where they live, they typically begin with the number of their *arrondissement*. Within these areas are recognised *quartiers*, or neighbourhoods, each of which has a distinctive character.

TRADITIONAL DIVIDES

According to an old saying, the Left Bank (south of the river) was where you did your thinking – the Sorbonne university has been located there since the Middle Ages – and the Right Bank (north of the river) was the place to spend money. Yet, in addition to this historic divide, there is a marked unofficial division between the traditionally working-class eastern end of the city and the mostly bourgeois west. In general, the further east you go, the further left you will also find yourself on the political spectrum. City planners have been struggling for decades to redress the social imbalance, culminating in urban-renewal projects around the Bastille *(see p.50)* and in Bercy *(see p.80)*.

POPULATION

Central Paris is more densely populated than London or New York, with its residents squeezed into tiny apartments in the city's 87 sq km (33.5 sq miles). A house and garden is an almost unheard-of luxury, and there is intense competition for desirable living space, with an average of 150,000 people looking for a home at any one time. High rents, especially in the western *arrondissements*, add to the fact that many Parisians have neither the time nor the money to appreciate the city they live in, being locked in a routine that they describe as *métro-boulot-dodo* (commuting, working, sleeping).

Nonetheless, for anyone who is fortunate enough to live in the city centre, the rewards far outweigh the demands. Human in scale, clean, comparatively safe, cosmopolitan and lively, Paris lives up to its reputation as one of the best cities on earth for living the good life.

CULTURAL SCENE

Paris dominates the country's art, literature, music, fashion, education, scientific research, commerce and politics, despite concerted attempts in recent years at decentralisation in France. It may not be good for the country as a whole, or for the provincial cities, but it adds to the cultural richness of life in the capital. Little wonder that the writer Jean Giraudoux (1882–1944) once claimed that the Parisian was more than a little proud to be part of a city where 'the most thinking, talking and writing in the world have been accomplished'.

Above from far left: access to the Grands Boulevards; in a Parisian park; old copies of *Vogue* on sale at a flea market; metro entrance.

Parisian Types
A French sociologist once claimed that in his country there were not three social classes but 63. One entrenched classification is BCBG *(bon chic, bon genre)*: the French equivalent of the British Sloane ranger or the American preppie. Their stomping grounds are the rich suburbs of the 16th and 17th *arrondissements*. Another taxonomic is *bobo (bourgeois bohème)*. These are the sort of 'bohemians' who can afford the high rents of St-Germain-des-Prés or the Marais.

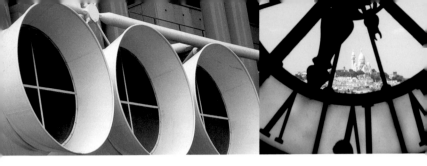

ARCHITECTURAL DEVELOPMENT

Largely undamaged by two world wars, Paris is the result of centuries of grandiose urban planning. It escaped only by a whisker during World War II, when General Dietrich von Cholhitz, the occupying governor of Paris, defied Hitler's orders to destroy every single historical edifice in the city as the Allied troops approached.

Gothic and Renaissance Styles

However, little remains of the city's architecture prior to the Gothic period. The 12th-century west front of Notre-Dame *(see p.26)* is a fine example of early Gothic, while the transept with

Right: Notre-Dame.

its intricate tracery and the interior of Sainte-Chapelle *(see p.25)* are excellent examples of mid-13th-century High Gothic.

In the mid-16th century, following campaigns in Italy, François I introduced grand Renaissance forms to the French capital. The best example of the French interpretation of the Renaissance style – known as Mannerism – is the palace at Fontainebleau *(see p.94)*.

Baroque and Neoclassicism

In the first half of the 17th century 60 new monasteries and 20 churches were built in the capital, with the aim of turning it into a second Rome. Churches such as Val-de-Grâce, in the 5th, were modelled on the Roman Baroque template with a two-storey gabled and pillared facade, a broad, barrel-vaulted nave flanked by chapels, and a high cupola above the crossing.

French art entered its classical phase in the reign of Louis XIV (1643–1715), notably with the palace of Versailles *(see p.90)*. Louis Le Vau, Jules Hardouin-Mansart and Charles Lebrun designed the exterior and interior of the palace, while landscape architect André Le Nôtre laid out the formal gardens.

The same team was appointed to oversee changes to the city, removing the city walls, replacing the old gates with triumphal arches, and redesigning place des Victoires and place Vendôme as royal squares with statues as centrepieces. The Louvre was extended, and the addition of the Tuileries and the Champs-Élysées created a 'Royal Axis' *(see p.30)*.

The 19th Century

The storming of the Bastille in 1789 heralded the start of the destruction of many churches during the years of revolution. However, Napoleon brought reconstruction and extended the Royal Axis by adding the Arc de Triomphe.

By the 1860s, though, a combination of neglect and rapid urban growth had made Paris more than ripe for redevelopment. Under town planner Baron Haussmann, the residential quarter of the city centre was pulled down, the street system transformed, and parks laid out on the city outskirts. The bourgeois pomp of the period reached its apogee in architect Charles Garnier's extravagant opera house *(see p.44)*, while mercantile success found expression in international exhibitions, notably that of 1889 which brought with it the Eiffel Tower *(see p.36)*.

Early 20th Century

The Modern Movement of the 1920s and 1930s and Art Deco, characterised by clean lines and stylised forms, were born in Paris, with architects Robert Mallet-Stevens and Le Corbusier their chief exponents. At the same time, a more grandiose, neoclassical form of Modernism emerged, epitomised by the Palais de Chaillot *(see p.71)*.

Later 20th Century

From the 1960s, Paris underwent a transformation. Facades were cleaned, the metro network modernised, and old parts of the city, such as the market at Les Halles *(see p.48)*, demolished. Technical advances enabled architects to build upwards (La Défense, *see p.86*), expand indoor space (Centre Pompidou, La Villette, Bercy, *see pp.46, 77 and 80*) and experiment with materials that reflect and admit light.

In the 1980s François Mitterrand left his mark with a number of *grands projets (see p.30)*. These include I.M. Pei's pyramidal entrance to the Louvre *(see p.30)*, Jean Nouvel's Institut du Monde Arabe, the Opéra Bastille *(see p.55)*, Grande Arche at La Défense *(see p.86)* and Bibliothèque Nationale de France – François Mitterrand *(see p.81)*.

The 21st Century

Recent years have brought Jacques Chirac's Musée du Quai Branly *(see p.38)*, the largest museum built in Paris since the Centre Pompidou. It seems, too, that the current president, Nicolas Sarkozy, intends to assure his legacy through architecture as well as infrastructure. His recently revealed 'Grand Paris' (Greater Paris) scheme kicked off with a pledge of €35 billion for a swish new suburban transport system, with 24-hour driverless trains connecting the suburbs and, notably, the airports to the centre of Paris. Sarkozy has also invited 10 world-class architects, including Jean Nouvel and Richard Rogers, to draw up their visions of a Greater Paris, with the aim of creating better harmony between the currently disjointed city centre and its suburbs. New monuments and skyscrapers (long banned in central Paris) are all possibilities for what will be a 10-year plan.

Above from far left: Centre Pompidou; a glimpse of Sacré-Coeur from the Musée d'Orsay; carousel in the Tuileries; at the Louvre

Above: Jardin des Plantes; Daniel Buren's columns, Palais Royal.

La Politesse

The widespread Parisian reputation for rudeness is largely undeserved; in fact, many locals follow strict rules of etiquette, and visitors are advised to follow the standard. Whether you are buying a baguette or shopping at Chanel, starting any transaction with a 'Bonjour Madame/ Monsieur' and finishing with 'Merci, au revoir', for example, should make the world of difference to the service you receive.

FOOD AND DRINK

French food is not all snails and frogs' legs. Its attractions include oysters, foie gras, boeuf bourguignon, steak tartare, coq-au-vin and sole meunière. And then comes dessert: tarte tatin, mousse au chocolat, ile flottante and more.

Salad
One of the joys of French cuisine is that a salad need not be a puritanically healthy affair. In the *salade Landaise* illustrated above, only a wisp of lettuce peeks out from under the mound of *charcuterie*.

Opposite: Maxim's restaurant *(see p.43).*
Below: fresh fish at the market.

Paris has the reputation of being one of the best cities in the world for food, with an illustrious gastronomic history. You may not find the most experimental dishes here, and the approach to food is admittedly far more conservative than, for example, in London or New York, but this is not without its benefits, especially for those visitors in search of classic French cuisine.

CONTEMPORARY AND INTERNATIONAL

This is not to say that contemporary and international cuisines cannot be found. In recent years, young chefs have been opening more fashion-conscious restaurants – impervious to Michelin ratings – serving French food, yet integrating (cautiously) more exotic flavours, such as ginger, peanut, curry and lime.

The international scene, although not as widespread as elsewhere, is also an integral part of the city's food culture. The greatest concentrations of Chinese and Vietnamese restaurants are in the 5th and 13th *arrondissements* (the Latin Quarter and southeast to the new Left Bank), while Japanese eateries are concentrated in the 1st (Louvre, Palais-Royal and Châtelet).

The best Moroccan restaurants are peppered across Paris, but around the Bastille is a good place to start. There is excellent Lebanese food in the 8th and 16th (Madeleine, Grands Boulevards, Champs-Élysées and West), while good African food can be found around Pigalle and the East.

PLACES TO EAT

Brasseries
Brasseries (breweries) were introduced to Paris in the 19th century, at about the time when modern methods of brewing were being perfected. They're a jolly experience: spacious, clamorous and convivial, usually exuberantly decorated in Belle Epoque style. Many serve Alsatian specialities, such as

choucroute and steins of beer; others specialise in seafood. Outside, you can usually see heaps of shellfish on beds of ice, and men in overalls shucking oysters from dawn till dusk. Usefully, unlike most other restaurants in Paris, brasseries generally remain open on Sundays.

Bistros

On the whole, bistros are smaller-scale establishments and mostly offer variations on a traditional repertoire of dishes including *hareng pommes à l'huile* (smoked herring marinated in oil with warm potatoes), *blanquette de veau* (veal in a white sauce), *mousse au chocolat* and *tarte tatin* (caramelised apple upside-down tart, *see p.17*). A number of bistros have a regional bent, and offer provincial specialities such as *foie gras* and duck (southwestern), hot pepper, salt cod and ham (Basque), and *bouillabaisse* (Provençale).

Cafés

These, in the traditional sense of the term, usually serve sandwiches, notably the ubiquitous *croque-monsieur* (grilled ham and cheese), as well as a variety of giant salads, quiches and omelettes. Some establishments offer fuller menus with a Mediterranean slant and more elaborate, modern dishes.

High-End Restaurants

Whether Michelin-starred or not, this category ranges from the gloriously old-fashioned, with truffle-studded *foie-gras* terrines and venison in grand sauces, to the self-consciously cutting-edge, with hot pepper sorbets to cleanse the palate between veal slow-cooked in orange juice and desserts that show off fruit or chocolate in five different ways. Such restaurants often have tasting menus *(dégustation)*.

Michelin stars are taken very seriously in France. At the time of printing, Paris had 14 restaurants with three stars, whereas London, for example, had only two, and New York had six. Losing a star can mean a sharp decline in the number of a restaurant's customers as well as a dent in the chef's pride. In 2003, just the fear of dropping a star after a less-than-perfect score from a critic led top chef Bernard Loiseau to take his own life.

Above from far left: a sweet treat; at the patisserie; smartly attired waiters.

Chef's Hat

The *toque blanche* (literally, 'white hat') is the name for the tall, round, pleated, starched hat worn by chefs across the world since the days of kitchen legend George Auguste Escoffier (1845–1935). Its multiple folds are supposed to signify the many ways that an egg can be cooked (usually there are exactly 100 pleats).

Cheese

The French eat more cheese than any other nation in the world: approximately 20.5kg (45lb) per person per year. Many cheeses taste a lot better than they look; some goats' cheeses *(illustrated above)*, for example, are coated in charcoal ash, as this absorbs surface moisture and helps preserve them.

Below: Le Petit Fer à Cheval *(see p.52)*, in the Marais.

Haute cuisine is also a costly affair, and not just for the customers. Running a first-class restaurant in France costs, on average, about 60 euros per customer, and even the best establishments have profit margins of only between two and five percent. Little wonder, therefore, that so many chefs look to endorsements of everything from saucepans to fish kettles.

CHEESE

Between the main course and dessert comes the cheese trolley or platter, laden with a delectably smelly array. There are two rules which may be helpful: 1) In a cheese tasting, always start with the mildest cheese and work your way around to the strongest; and 2) Never steal 'the nose' off a piece of cheese if you're serving yourself; always slice cheese in such a way as to preserve its natural shape. This is considered proper behaviour, since it means that the last person served will not be left with just the rind.

Varieties

The number of varieties means that it can take years to become familiar with French cheeses. President Charles de Gaulle once said, 'how can you govern a country that has 246 different kinds of cheese?' In fact, cheese in France is as regulated a produce as wine, with a similar Appellation d'Origine Contrôlée (AOC) classification system, as well as a protected 'Designation of Origin'. There are now more than 40 cheeses with AOC status (Roquefort was the first, in 1925), and in total somewhere from 350 to 400 varieties of French cheese.

DRINKS

Alcoholic Beverages

It is common to be offered an *apéritif*, such as a glass of Champagne, white wine, a kir (white wine with the blackcurrant liqueur, cassis) or sometimes white port, before a meal in France.

Wine is the ever-present accompaniment to eating, though, whether by the bottle, by the glass or, cheaply, by the jug. In bistros, brasseries and cafés, though often not in formal restau-

rants, house wine can be ordered in *carafes* or *pichets* (earthernware jugs). Quantities are normally 25cl *(un quart)*, 50cl *(un demi)*, or sometimes 46cl *(un pot lyonnais)*.

The current trend in France is to drink less wine, but of better quality. The interest in organic wine has also mushroomed – Cyril Bordarier's Le Verre Volé, by the Canal St-Martin, is a *cave à manger* (a fashionable cross between a wine cellar and restaurant), specialising in organic wines; Olivier Camus's Le Chapeau Melon, in Belleville, is a former wine shop-turned-restaurant where *vins naturels* are the order of the day. Recent years have seen a growth in Parisian restaurants focusing on wine, championed by Il Vino (www.ilvinobyenricobernardo. com), which was awarded a Michelin star just three months after opening. Female sommeliers such as Nathalie and Robin at Le Garde-Robe have been making waves, too.

France constantly vies with Italy for the title of world's largest wine producer, and two-thirds of the annual production of 600 million cases is consumed in France; expect, therefore, to find relatively few bottles from overseas on restaurant wine lists.

Beer is usually only ordered with sandwiches, Alsatian meals or Asian food. Cider accompanies Breton and Norman specialities such as *crêpes* or mussels, and is often served in earthenware beakers.

After dinner comes the *digestif*, which may be a glass of Cognac, Armagnac, Calvados or distilled fruit liqueur.

Soft Drinks and Coffee

Numerous mineral waters will be on offer in most restaurants. Request *pétillante* for sparkling; *plate* for still; or *en carafe*, if you are happy with a jug of tap water.

Coffee in France is usually served after, rather than with, dessert. *Café* means espresso, strong and black. If you like milk, request a *café noisette*. *Café crème* (coffee with milk) is considered a breakfast drink; ordering it after dinner may raise eyebrows. Finally, if caffeine is likely to keep you up all night, ask for a *café décaféiné* (*déca* for short), or for *une tisane* (herbal tea).

Above from far left: Paris is a cheese lover's dream; wine shop wares; tarte tatin.

Did You Know? The tarte tatin *(shown above)* is named after the Tatin sisters, who invented it by accident at their country hotel in 1889, after a conventional apple pie they were cooking went wrong.

Markets

In general, visiting Parisian food markets is a morning activity, with stalls opening at 9am and packing up at 1pm. Of the daily street markets, the Marché d'Aligre (place d'Aligre, 12th *arrondissement*) has an indoor part (the 'Marché Beauvau') with produce of the highest quality (and price), as well as a noisier, cheaper outside section. Then there is the market on rue Mouffetard in the Latin Quarter: look out for the Italian delicatessen, Facchetti, and Steff the baker. Among the roving markets are Breteuil (starting from place de Breteuil in the 7th; Tue and Sat), with specialists in snails, wild strawberries and foie gras; Bastille (flowing from place de la Bastille, in the 11th, up boulevard Richard-Lenoir; Thur and Sun), with stands devoted solely to onions, mushrooms, honey or eggs; and Belleville-Ménilmontant (boulevard de Belleville to boulevard de Ménilmontant on the border of the 11th and the 20th; Tue and Fri), with exotic varieties of peppers, giant watermelons, Chinese cabbages, figs the size of fists and flatbreads made from rye or barley.

SHOPPING

While Napoleon once branded Britain 'a nation of shopkeepers', nowadays the phrase is more aptly applied to France, and viewed not as an insult but as a compliment for the wonderful array of one-off specialist boutiques and stores.

Opening Times
Most shops open from 9 or 10am until around 7pm. Few stores open on Sunday, except in the Marais and a few on the Champs-Élysées. Some smaller shops close on Monday all day or in the morning until about 2pm. Many close throughout August for the traditional French summer holiday. The main sales *(soldes)* periods in France are January and July.

In an age when shopping seems to be an increasingly uniform experience wherever you are, with the same international groups and luxury labels in every major city around the world, Paris still retains its tradition of family-owned specialist shops, and chain stores and *centres commerciaux* (shopping malls) are far less prevalent here than in most other European capitals.

THE SHOPPING MAP

The city's different *quartiers* each have their own mood and atmosphere, and their shops often reflect the history and type of people who live there. Expect to find shops selling classic and expensive items (antiques and up-market interior design as well as fashion labels, for example) in the wealthy, fairly conservative 7th and 16th *arrondissements*, and bohemian designers and independent gift shops and boutiques on the hilly streets of Montmartre (rue des Abbesses, for example), in the fashionable Bastille and Marais and dotted along the banks of the Canal St-Martin.

Couture and Chains
The city's big couture houses are clustered mostly in the avenue Montaigne area (off the Champs-Élysées), the

Faubourg St-Honoré and St-Germain. However, the once-staid rue St-Honoré has become the focus for a more avant-garde fashion set, thanks to the establishment here of Colette, the original lifestyle store. Even the exclusive avenue Montaigne has tempered its bourgeois image with the arrival of hip young labels Paul & Joe and Zadig & Voltaire; all of which has had the knock-on effect of attracting other cool boutiques and gift shops to the area.

Tradition and Change
Emblematic of glamour in the early part of the 20th century, the Champs-Élysées nose-dived to tourist dross in the 1980s. Its return to favour at the end of the 1990s was confirmed by the arrival here of *pâtissier extraordinaire*, Ladurée *(see p.43)*, and in the last few years the avenue has been boosted by a swathe of swish concept stores.

In the past decade, designer stores have migrated to St-Germain, much to the chagrin of those who bemoan the loss of the district's distinguished booksellers and literary cachet.

Regeneration is now under way around the widely disliked Forum des Halles shopping centre. After a number of years the Mairie de Paris

has decided on a design to redevelop the Forum; a huge glass canopy will cover re-landscaped squares and gardens. The project has an estimated completion date of 2012.

Not that every area is in the throes of regeneration. The aristocratic past of boulevards Bonne Nouvelle and Montmartre is a dim memory blurred by the ranks of discount stores and high-street chains that now dominate the area. That said, the department stores, or *grands magasins*, built in the 19th century, still hold their own and look as impressive as ever.

GALLERIES AND PASSAGES

In the 1840s Paris had over 100 passages, or covered arcades, built with shops below and living quarters above. They were places for Parisians to discover novelties and the latest fashions, while protected from the elements. Nowadays there are only around 20 left, mostly near the Palais Royal. The passages usually open from around 7am to 9 or 10pm, and are locked at night and on Sunday.

Highlights
The best-preserved gallery, **Galerie Vivienne** (6 rue Vivienne, 2nd; metro: Bourse), has a beautiful mosaic floor and gorgeous iron-and-glass roof. This fashionable spot is home to the ateliers-boutiques of Jean-Paul Gaultier and Nathalie Garçon, art galleries and the genteel A Priori tearoom.
Galerie Véro-Dodat (19 rue Jean-Jacques Rousseau–2 rue du Bouloi,

1st; metro: Palais-Royal Musée du Louvre) dates from 1826 and is perhaps the finest of the passages, with wood-and-brass shop fronts and carved Corinthian capitals. Highlights include antique dolls at Robert Capia, leather goods at Il Bisonte and bespoke make-up at By Terry.
Passage du Grand Cerf (10 rue Dussoubs or 145 rue St-Denis, 2nd; metro: Étienne Marcel) is probably the coolest of the arcades – something of a creative headquarters. Come here for work by cutting-edge graphic designers, milliners and jewellers.
Passage des Panoramas (10 rue St-Marc or 11 boulevard Montmartre, 2nd; metro: Bourse) is one of the earliest of the arcades, opened in 1800, and above all a focus for philatelists, with half a dozen specialist stamp dealers.

HISTORY: KEY DATES

The Parisii tribe discovered it, the Romans usurped it, the Franks invaded it and Napoleon ruled it. The city's refined culture and revolutionary politics changed the world. The list below covers major, mostly political, events.

EARLY HISTORY

Key Dates: Kings and Emperors
Charlemagne
(768–814)
Hugues Capet
(987–996)
Louis IX (1226–70)
François I (1515–47)
Henri II (1547–59)
Henri III (1574–89)
Henri IV (1589–1610)
Louis XIV
(1643–1715; *above*)
Louis XV (1715–74)
Louis XVI (1774–93)
Louis-Philippe of
Orléans (1830–48)

c. 300 BC	Celtic Parisii tribe settle on the Île de la Cité and found Lutétia.
58–52 BC	Paris conquered by the Romans; building on the Left Bank.
c. AD 250	St-Denis establishes the first Christian community in Paris.
451	St-Geneviève saves Paris from Attila the Hun.
508	Clovis, King of Franks, makes Paris his capital.

THE MIDDLE AGES

768–814	Carolingian dynasty. Power shifted from Paris to Aix-la-Chapelle.
987	Hugues Capet is elected king; start of Capetian rule.
1246–8	Louis IX builds Sainte-Chapelle.
1253	Founding of the Sorbonne.
1340	Hundred Years' War begins.
1420	Paris surrendered to the English, who rule until 1436.

RENAISSANCE AND ENLIGHTENMENT

1469	First French printworks.
1515–47	Reign of François I, during which he starts to rebuild the Louvre.
1589	Henri III is assassinated.
1594	Henri IV converts to Catholicism, ending the Wars of Religion.
1631	Launch of the first Paris newspaper, *La Gazette*.
1667	First street lighting in Paris.
1682	Louis XIV moves his court to Versailles.

REVOLUTION, EMPIRE AND REPUBLIC

1789	French Revolution ends centuries of monarchy in France. The First Republic is established in its place. Louis XVI and Marie-Antoinette are executed in 1793.
1794	The ensuing Terror claims more than 60,000 lives.

1799	Napoleon Bonaparte seizes power and is crowned emperor in 1804.
1814–15	Fall of Napoleon heralds the restoration of the Bourbon monarchy.
1830	Bourgeois revolution; Louis-Philippe of Orléans becomes king.
1848	Revolution brings Louis-Napoleon, nephew of Bonaparte, to power, and ushers in the Second Republic.
1852	Louis-Napoleon crowns himself Napoleon III: the Second Empire. Baron Georges Haussmann begins an 18-year redesign of the city. The city's first department store, Le Bon Marché, opens.
1870–1	Franco-Prussian War. Paris surrenders. Napoleon III abdicates. End of the Second Empire. The Third Republic lasts till 1940.
1871	Uprising by the Paris Commune, with 25,000 people killed.
1889	Eiffel Tower built for the World Fair. Pigalle's Moulin Rouge opens.

Above from far left: the taking of the Bastille; boulevard Haussmann around the turn of the 20th century.

20TH CENTURY

1900	First Paris metro line opens.
1914–18	World War I.
1934	The Depression gives rise to riots and a series of strikes.
1939–45	World War II. France falls to the Nazis in June 1940.
1946	Charles de Gaulle founds the Fourth Republic.
1958	Algerian crisis topples the Fourth Republic. De Gaulle founds the Fifth Republic. Women are finally given the vote.
1962	End of the Algerian War.
1968	Student riots and workers' general strikes rock Paris and force de Gaulle to call an election. He wins but resigns a year later.
1969–74	Georges Pompidou's presidency.
1974–81	Valéry Giscard d'Estaing's presidency.
1981–95	Mitterrand's presidency is notable for his architectural *grands projets*.
1998	France wins the football World Cup, hosted in Paris.

Above: bust of Gustave Eiffel by his namesake tower.

21ST CENTURY

2001	Bertrand Delanoë is elected mayor of Paris.
2002	The euro replaces the franc as the French unit of currency.
2005	Urban unrest over immigration and racism in Paris.
2006	New tram service in the south of the city.
2007	Presidential election won by right-wing candidate Nicolas Sarkozy.
2010	President Sarkozy unveils his plans to create a 'Greater Paris' *(see p.13)*.
2011	European Athletics Indoor Championships held at the Palais Omnisports de Paris Bercy in March.
2012	Presidential elections due.

Recent Presidents
Charles de Gaulle (1958–69)
Georges Pompidou (1969–74)
Valéry Giscard d'Estaing (1974–81)
François Mitterrand (1981–95)
Jacques Chirac (1995–2007)
Nicolas Sarkozy (2007–)

WALKS AND TOURS

THE ISLANDS

The two largest islands in the Seine – the Île de la Cité and the Île St-Louis – offer up the full span of the history of Paris, via some of its greatest sights: the Pont Neuf, Notre-Dame, Conciergerie and Sainte-Chapelle.

DISTANCE 2km (1¼ miles)
TIME Two or three hours
START Pont Neuf
END Île St-Louis
POINTS TO NOTE
Do the tour early in the morning to try to avoid the crowds at Notre-Dame.

It was on the Île de la Cité, the largest island in the Seine, that the city of Paris was founded, when the Celtic tribe of the Parisii built their first huts there in the 3rd century BC. The island remains the geographical centre of the capital, though the focus nowadays is tourism, due mainly to Notre-Dame cathedral.

PONT NEUF

The tour starts on the **Pont Neuf ❶**, which, despite its name (New Bridge), is actually the city's oldest. Henri III laid the first stone in 1578; Henri IV inaugurated the completed bridge in 1607.

Statue of Henri IV

As you walk south across the bridge, note the equestrian statue of Henri IV. Originally produced in 1614 under the orders of Marie de Médicis, Henri's widow, it was destroyed in 1792 during the Revolution, then rebuilt in 1818 on the monarchy's restoration. This statue was made from the original cast using two statues of Napoleon as raw material.

Recently, restoration experts X-raying the statue to check for cracks have discovered that the caster, a fervent Bonapartiste, had enclosed a small statue of his hero intact inside the big one. He also hid inside the statue four boxes containing a history of the life of Henri IV, a 17th-century parchment certifying the original statue, a description of how the new statue had been

Quai des Orfèvres
The police headquarters and home to the fictional character Maigret is generally referred to by its address. Since 1946 it has lent its name to a literary prize for detective novels. The prize's jury is made up of real detectives.

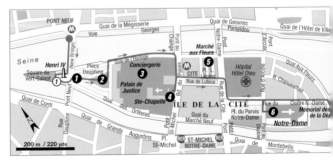

Above from far left: Notre-Dame; bars at the Conciergerie; St-Louis-en-l'Île; out for a stroll on the Île St-Louis.

commissioned and a list of contributors to the public subscription.

Behind the statue are stairs leading to **square du Vert-Galant**, a tiny patch with views across to the Louvre and a good place for a picnic. Across the road is the **Taverne Henri IV**, see ①①.

PLACE DAUPHINE

Adjacent to the Taverne Henri IV is an opening on to **place Dauphine ❷**. This square was commissioned by Henri IV in 1607 in honour of his son, the dauphin Louis (later Louis XIII), and intended as a market for traders. It now comprises 32 elegant white-stone townhouses constructed around a triangular courtyard. Famous past residents have included the singer Yves Montand.

Cross the square and turn left on to the quai de l'Horloge, named after the city's first public clock, which is on a tower of the Conciergerie.

CONCIERGERIE

The **Conciergerie ❸** (2 boulevard du Palais; tel: 01 53 40 60 80; www. conciergerie.monuments-nationaux.fr;

daily Mar–Oct 9.30am–6pm, Nov–Feb 9am–5pm; charge) was originally part of the palace of King Philippe the Fair (1268–1314), but soon became the residence of the keeper of the royal palaces or *comte des cierges* (keeper of the seals), from which the word *concierge* is derived.

The building was later transformed into a prison, and it was here that in 1793, in the Reign of Terror, around 2,600 of the condemned spent their last night before facing the guillotine. Now a museum, the Conciergerie has a guillotine blade on display, as well as the crucifix Marie-Antoinette used at prayer when in captivity here, and the lock from Robespierre's cell.

SAINTE-CHAPELLE

Concealed in the courtyard between the Conciergerie and Palais de Justice (the French supreme court) is the Gothic **Sainte-Chapelle ❹** (4 boulevard du Palais; tel: 01 53 40 60 80; www.sainte-chapelle.monuments-nationaux.fr; daily Mar–Oct 9.30am–6pm, Nov–Feb 9am–5pm; charge). The chapel was constructed in the 13th century to house holy relics,

Pont Neuf
The bridge owes its survival to its stone, rather than wooden, construction, and because it was built without houses on it (though shops were added later). The structure has never been altered. In 1985 Bulgarian-born artist Christo and his partner Jeanne-Claude, with the help of 300 employees, wrapped the bridge (individually wrapping even the lamp-posts) in 40,876 sq m (439, 985 sq ft) of fabric.

QUAI D'ORLÉANS

Food and Drink 🍴

① TAVERNE HENRI IV
13 place du Pont-Neuf, 1st; tel: 01 43 54 27 90; €
Diminutive spot on the tip of the Île de la Cité offering straightforward French cuisine and excellent wines. Try the eggs baked with blue cheese and ham, washed down with a white Beaujolais. Excellent value given the high-profile location.

[map of Île St-Louis area showing: Rue de l'Hôtel de Ville, R. des Lions St-Paul, PONT MARIE, Quai des Célestins, Voie Georges Pompidou, SULLY MORLAND, de Bourbon, Hôtel du Jeu de Paume, Hôtel Lauzun, Hôtel Lambert, ❾, Quai d'Anjou, Quai Henri IV, St-Louis-en-l'Île ❽, Hôtel Chenizot, Pont de Sully, Barye, ÎLE ST-LOUIS, Quai de Béthune, Pont de la Tournelle, d'Orléans, Rue la Régrattier, Quai d'Orléans, Seine]

including Christ's Crown of Thorns, bought by the pious Louis IX (later St-Louis) from the Venetians at a price more than three times the cost of the building itself.

Enter via the lower chapel, which was used by palace servants. Note the star-patterned ceiling. Stairs lead to the upper chapel, where light blazes through 15m (49ft) -high stained-glass windows separated by the slimmest of buttresses. Those interested in chamber music should check the bulletin boards for concert schedules.

MARCHÉ AUX FLEURS

Cross the road to place Louis Lépine. Here, at the **Marché aux Fleurs** ❺, flower-sellers ply their trade from Monday to Saturday, while on Sundays caged-bird sellers take their place. Continuing east across rue de la Cité is the **Hôtel Dieu**, the oldest hospital in Paris. Founded in the 7th century, it was rebuilt by Baron Haussmann in the 1860s. Adjacent is place du Parvis Notre-Dame, in front of the cathedral.

NOTRE-DAME

The building of **Notre-Dame** ❻ (place du Parvis Notre-Dame, 4th; tel: 01 42 34 56 10; www.notredamedeparis.com; Mon–Fri 8am–6.45pm, Sat–Sun 8am–7.15pm; free except Treasury, Crypt and Tower) was initiated by Bishop Sully in 1163, and took almost 200 years to complete. In the centuries since, it has witnessed medieval executions, conversion to a food warehouse during the

Revolution, the coronation of Emperor Napoleon in 1804, and the service marking the Liberation of Paris in 1944 (interrupted by sniping and wounding of several of the congregation).

Enter the cathedral through one of the three sculpted Gothic portals recounting stories from the scriptures and lives of the saints for the illiterate masses. Above are statues of 28 kings of Judea – all replicas, since most were destroyed during the Revolution when they were mistaken for French kings. Several originals were rediscovered in 1977 and are on display in the Musée National du Moyen Age *(see p.59)*.

Inside, 29 chapels line the nave, transept and choir. The rose windows, 43ft (13m) in diameter, date from 1250–70, though they have been extensively restored. The *Pietà* on the large altar at the far end of the cathedral was commissioned by Louis XIII in thanks for the birth of his son and heir.

Treasury, Crypt and Bell Tower

The **Treasury** (Mon–Fri 9.30am–6pm, Sat 9.30am–6.30pm, Sun 1.30–6.30pm; charge), off the south aisle to the right of the High Altar, displays religious relics, robes and jewelled chalices. The **Crypt** (Tue–Sun 10am–6pm; charge) focuses on archaeological finds. As you leave the church, you will see signs to the **Bell Tower** (daily Apr–Sept 10am–6.30pm, June–Aug Sat–Sun until 11pm, Oct–Mar 10am–5.30pm; charge). The 82m (270ft) spiralling ascent takes you to Quasimodo's huge brass bell and brings you face to face with the gargoyles.

Stained Glass
In Sainte-Chapelle's upper chapel there are 85 major window panels, depicting 1,134 biblical scenes, of which 720 are 13th-century originals. During the Revolution the chapel became an administrative office, with huge filing cabinets blocking the windows. Ironically, this helped them to survive: the choir stalls, rood screen and even the spire were destroyed. The chapel was restored in the 19th century.

Kilomètre Zéro
Look out among the cobbles of place du Parvis Notre-Dame for the round marker that marks 'Kilomètre Zéro', the point from which distances in France are all traditionally measured.

East of the cathedral is the **Mémorial des Martyrs de la Déportation ❼** (daily 10am–noon and 2–5pm, till 7pm in summer; free), a monument to those deported to German concentration camps in World War II.

ÎLE ST-LOUIS

From the memorial, take the pedestrian bridge to the **Île St-Louis**. Follow rue St-Louis-en-l'Île along the spine of the island past a succession of grand mansions interspersed with boutiques and restaurants, including **Mon Vieil Ami**, see ⑪②. The Hôtel du Jeu de Paume at no. 54 was once a real tennis court. Hôtel Chenizot at no. 51 has a splendid rocaille doorway with bearded fauns, and a balcony supported by dragons.

When you reach rue des Deux Ponts, turn right for a moment to see the **Pont de la Tournelle** with Landowski's 1928 Art Nouveau statue of the patron saint of Paris, St Geneviève, commemorating a river journey that she made to find food for the starving citizens of Paris.

Back on rue St-Louis-en-l'Île, you soon come to the Baroque church of **St-Louis-en-l'Île ❽**. Designed by Louis Le Vau in the 1660s, it is notable for its open-work spire, iron clock and 16th- and 17th-century artworks.

Island of Cows

Perpendicular to rue St-Louis-en-l'Île is rue Poulletier (formerly Poultier), once a fortified canal, with the area beyond having been a boggy pasture known as the 'Island of Cows'. It was filled in after a property developer persuaded Louis XIII in 1614 to transform the island into an elegant residential quarter. At the end of rue St-Louis-en-l'Île, at no. 2, is the Hôtel Lambert, built by Le Vau in 1641 for Louis XIII's secretary. Here, Voltaire enjoyed a tempestuous love affair with the lady of the house, the Marquise du Châtelet.

Quai d'Anjou

Now turn left and double back on yourself to find the **Hôtel Lauzun ❾**, at 17 quai d'Anjou. Built in 1640 by Le Vau and now owned by the Rothschilds, the mansion was home in 1845 to the poets Théophile Gautier and Charles Baudelaire. They kept a salon on the second floor for their Hashish Eaters' Club, and Baudelaire wrote his collection *Les Fleurs du Mal* in the house.

Finishing the tour here, turn right and cross Pont Marie to the metro. Alternatively, if you are in need of refreshment, pop into **Berthillon**, see ⑪③, for their much-fêted ice cream.

Above from far left: Notre-Dame's west front; Sainte-Chapelle's starry lower chapel.

Barye Monument
At the end of the Île St-Louis, like the stern of a ship, is a small park and monument dedicated to Antoine-Louis Barye (1796–1875), a sculptor famous for his bronzes of animals.

Food and Drink 🍴

② MON VIEIL AMI
69 rue St-Louis-en-l'Île, 4th; tel: 01 40 46 01 35; closed Mon–Tue; €€€
Fine cooking with an Alsatian accent. Signature dishes include *pâté en croûte* and shoulder of roebuck. Lavish medieval dining room.

③ GLACIER BERTHILLON
29–31 rue St-Louis-en-l'Île, 4th; tel: 01 43 54 31 61; closed Mon–Tue; €
Parisian ice-cream institution (est. 1954) with an attractive tearoom next door.

LOUVRE AND TUILERIES

The Louvre is arguably the most famous museum in the world, with claims to being the largest. There are 35,000 pieces of art on display (from a collection of 300,000) in 6ha (15 acres) of exhibition space, so after your visit you may need to rest on a deckchair in the pretty Tuileries gardens.

Above: the stylish Café Marly faces on to the Louvre's main courtyard.

DISTANCE 1.5km (1 mile), not incl. distance covered in museum
TIME A full day
START Louvre
END Jeu de Paume
POINTS TO NOTE

If the Pyramid entrance to the museum is congested, enter instead at 99 rue de Rivoli via the Carrousel du Louvre shopping centre, or directly from the metro. With a Paris Museum Pass *(see margin opposite)*, you can go in via the Porte des Lions entrance. Tickets are valid all day, which allows re-entry into the museum after a rest in a café or restaurant (or even the Tuileries) outside the complex. Note that entry is free on the first Sunday of the month.

This tour incorporates a morning in the **Musée du Louvre ❶** (rue du Louvre; tel: 01 40 20 50 50; www.louvre.fr; Thur and Sat–Mon 9am–6pm, Wed and Fri 9am–10pm; charge except first Sun of month and 14 July), followed by an afternoon in the adjacent Tuileries gardens. If you need somewhere to have breakfast, try the **Café Marly**, see ⑪①, or, if you're visiting later in the day, **Le Fumoir** or the **Garde-Robe**, see ⑪② and ⑪③. But first some background…

LOUVRE BACKGROUND

Originally built as a fortress in 1190 by King Philippe-Auguste to protect a weak link in the city wall, the Louvre was transformed into a royal château in the 1360s by Charles V, who established

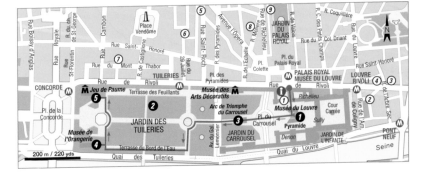

his extensive library in one of the towers. Sections of the palace were demolished, rebuilt or extended by successive monarchs, including François I, who in 1516 invited Leonardo da Vinci to be his court painter; the Italian brought with him his masterpieces the *Mona Lisa* and *The Virgin of the Rocks*, now highlights of the museum's collection. In 1682, however, the Louvre's period as a royal palace came to an end, as Louis XIV decamped entirely to Versailles.

Artists Move In

Following the court's departure, a colony of painters and sculptors moved into the Louvre's empty halls and corridors; among them was Guillaume Coustou, sculptor of the *Marly Horses*, now one of the Louvre's most prized exhibits.

During the 18th century, the fine arts academy, which had joined the Académie Française and other academic bodies in the royal apartments, organised exhibitions in the Salon Carré for artists to exhibit their work. This became the tradition known as the 'Salon' and lasted for over 120 years.

Public Museum

During the 18th-century Revolution, in a moment of artistic enthusiasm, the Assemblée Nationale decided to inaugurate the palace as a museum, ironically fulfilling the plans of Louis XVI, the king they had just beheaded. Opened in August 1793, the museum exhibited the collections of the royal family and of aristocrats who had fled abroad. These were augmented by Napoleon's efforts to relocate much of Europe's artistic wealth here following his victorious military campaigns in Italy, Austria and Germany. After Napoleon was defeated at the Battle of Waterloo in 1815, many of the stolen masterpieces were reclaimed by their rightful owners, but many more remained.

The rest of the 19th century and the first half of the 20th century brought with them periodic upheavals, notably the 1830 and 1848 revolutions, the Franco-Prussian War, the Paris Commune and two world wars, yet the Louvre continued to expand its collections and gradually came to occupy the whole of the vast complex of buildings.

Above from far left: inside the Louvre; old and new faces of the museum.

Food and Drink 🍴

① CAFÉ MARLY

93 rue de Rivoli, cour Napoléon du Louvre, 1st; tel: 01 49 26 06 60; €€
Open all day every day and particularly good for breakfast. Sit on the terrace overlooking the glass pyramid or enjoy the plush interior.

② LE FUMOIR

6 rue de l'Amiral-de-Coligny, 1st; tel: 01 42 92 00 24; €€
This 'smoking room' feels more like a club than a bar. Regulars sit in squishy leather seats while sipping Mojitos and perusing something from the 3,000-plus library or the newspaper rack.

③ LA GARDE-ROBE

41 rue de l'Arbre Sec, 1st; tel: 01 49 26 90 60; closed Sun–Tue; €
The 'wardrobe' is a tiny bar near the Louvre, with two acclaimed sommeliers, Nathalie and Robin. The walls are lined with bottles, and there are around 200 different wines here, most of which are available by the glass. Food is available in the form of cheese, ham or oyster platters.

Museum Pass

If you plan to visit several museums during your stay, buying a Paris Museum Pass enables you to avoid the queues and save money on entrance prices at over 60 museums and monuments in Paris and the Île-de-France region; you can also make unlimited visits within the time allowed. Cards are available for two, four or six days (at time of printing, €32, €48 and €64, respectively) and can be purchased from tourist offices, museums and galleries, at the airports and online. For further details, visit www.paris museumpass.com.

Grand Projects

The culmination of this process came in 1981, when President François Mitterrand commissioned a massive renovation of the Louvre, as one of his 'grands projets'. In addition to the Louvre renovation, these major architectural projects, which were completed in the 1980s and 1990s, included the construction of six new attractions (La Villette's Cité des Sciences, the riverside Institut du Monde Arabe, the Grande Arche at La Défense, the Opéra Bastille, the Finance Ministry at Bercy and Tolbiac's Bibliothèque Nationale François Mitterrand), plus the conversion of the Gare d'Orsay into the Musée d'Orsay.

When it was finished, the so-called 'Grand Louvre' had doubled in size, giving it claim to being the world's biggest museum, with 6ha (15 acres) of exhibition space. It also became the world's most visited museum, with more than 8 million visitors per year.

The Pyramid

The controversial Louvre pyramid, designed by Sino-American architect I.M. Pei, opened in 1989. The new addition reflects and, to some minds, complements the ancient curves of the surrounding buildings. However, to traditionalists such modernism amid heritage is heresy. Some detractors even ascribed a 'Pharaonic complex' to Mitterrand (he was already nicknamed 'the Sphinx' due to his enigmatic manner).

But the pyramid was not just designed to dazzle. It also allows light to flood into the new sunken court housing the main ticket desks and, along with three smaller pyramids, illuminates the area where shops, restaurants, cafés and an exhibition area are situated.

TOUR OF THE MUSEUM

The museum itself is divided into three wings: **Richelieu** in the north, **Sully** in the east and **Denon** in the south. The collections are displayed in colour-coded sections, to help with orientation, and excellent floor plans are also available at the ticket desks. The following is a brief tour, showing what is displayed where, including information on the highlights from the different sections.

The Medieval Louvre

You start at the lower ground floor of the Sully Wing, where the remains of Philippe-Auguste's fort and keep built in 1190 are on show, as well as some of the artefacts discovered in excavations in the 1980s. Drawings and scale models show the Louvre at different stages of its evolution, and reveal how many transformations it has undergone.

Walk around the medieval walls and fortress, past towers that were once the gates to the city. Of the artefacts uncovered in the excavations, the most impressive is Charles VI's helmet, which has been rebuilt from barely recognisable fragments and is on display in the Salle St-Louis.

Egyptian and Classical Antiquities and Italian Sculpture

At this point head upstairs to the ground and first floors of the Sully

Pyramid Points
The pyramid forms part of the Royal Axis, or Triumphal Way, an alignment of monuments, regal and triumphal, leading from the Louvre's Cour Carrée via the Arc de Triomphe du Carrousel and Arc de Triomphe to the Grande Arche in La Défense. Contrary to popular myth, its steel structure does not contain the satanic number of 666 panes of glass, but 673 segments, 603 of which are rhombus-shaped and 70 triangular.

Wing, home to Egyptian and Greek antiquities. The showpiece here, in room 13, is the 2nd-century BC *Venus de Milo (see right)*.

For Etruscan and Roman antiquities, make your way to the ground floor of the Denon wing. This is also the showcase for later Italian sculpture, including Michelangelo's *Dying Slave* and Canova's neoclassical *Psyche and Cupid* (1793).

French Sculpture

For French sculpture, aim for the Richelieu Wing, where such works as Guillaume Coustou's *Marly Horses* are displayed on the lower ground floor. On the ground floor, the French sculpture collection continues, with works spanning the 5th to 18th centuries. Also located here are Mesopotamian finds such as the black basalt Babylonian Code of Hammurabi (1792–1750 BC), which is one of the world's first legal documents.

French Masterpieces

The first floor exhibits some of the Western world's most iconic images. In the Denon Wing are some spectacular large-format French paintings, notably Eugène Delacroix's *Liberty Leading the People*, Théodore Géricault's *Raft of the Medusa* and Jacques-Louis David's *Consecration of Napoleon*. This last picture shows the scene in Notre-Dame at which Napoleon is said to have snubbed the Pope and crowned himself emperor, before crowning Josephine too.

Mona Lisa

Adjacent is a room that is dedicated to Leonardo da Vinci's enigmatic Florentine noblewoman, the *Mona Lisa* (entitled *La Joconde*, in French, after the name of her husband: Francesco del Giocondo). This 16th-century portrait was bought into France by François I, when the artist came to work at his court *(see p.94)*; in the 1980s it was attacked and is therefore now pro-

Above from far left: palatial decor; antique Napoleon pipe on sale in the Louvre des Antiquaires, next to the museum; photographing the art.

Venus de Milo
With her serene gaze, soft curves and naturalistic drapery, the Venus de Milo was discovered, minus her arms, on the island of Milos in 1820 and promptly purchased by the French government for 6,000 francs. The sensuous statue has been identified as Aphrodite, the Greek goddess of love and beauty, who is often represented half naked, and was probably inspired by the works of Praxiteles. Working in the mid-4th century BC, the Greek sculptor was a forerunner of Hellenistic art, and his nude interpretations of gods and goddesses were often copied.

Left: Canova's *Cupid and Psyche*.

Above from left: portrait of François I; *Winged Victory of Samothrace*; flowers and modern sculpture in the Tuileries.

tected by bullet-proof glass. Hanging alongside is Paolo Veronese's *Wedding at Cana*, where Jesus is said to have turned water into wine.

Other First-Floor Highlights

At the staircase dividing the Denon and Sully wings is the *Winged Victory of Samothrace* (2nd century BC), a Hellenistic figurehead commemorating a victory at sea, and the glittering Galerie d'Apollon (Apollo's Gallery), which holds the crown jewels. Note also the gallery's elaborate ceiling by Eugène Delacroix. The first floor of the Richelieu Wing contains Napoleon III's apartments, which now display works of the decorative arts.

French and Dutch Painting

The whole of the second floor is devoted to painting, with highlights including Dürer's *Self-Portrait*, Vermeer's *The Lacemaker*, Watteau's *Pierrot* and Ingres' *The Turkish Bath*. Look out for the Rubens Room, devoted to the 24 pictures produced between 1622 and 1625 for Marie de Médicis, illustrating the principal events in her life.

Stealing the *Mona Lisa*

On a Monday morning in August 1911, someone walked into the Salon Carré, lifted the *Mona Lisa* off the wall and made off with it. Remarkably, it wasn't until Tuesday at noon that its absence was noted. Within hours 160 policemen swarmed the museum, which was then shut for a week. Rumours circulated; even the directors were suspected of staging the theft to boost attendance. The painting's case was found in a stairwell and a thumb print discovered on its glass; sadly, this was useless, since it was a left thumb print, and the police only kept records of right ones.

For two years nothing was heard. Then, in November 1913, a young man approached an antiques dealer in Florence. Introducing himself as Vincenzo Leonard, and an Italian patriot, he said he had brought the *Mona Lisa* back to Italy. He requested a reward of 500,000 lire. The dealer called the Director of the Uffizi Gallery, and together they went to view the painting in the man's hotel room. Under the false bottom of a trunk there it was, perfectly preserved. While the painting was taken to the Uffizi for authentication, the man waited at his hotel. Police soon arrived and arrested him, under his real name, Vincenzo Perugia. After a triumphal tour of Italy, the painting was returned to Paris. The thief was tried in Florence, where he gained popularity as a patriot: given the minimum sentence, he was released almost immediately for time already served.

Artworks are still stolen from the Louvre every so often (a Corot in 1998, a marble statue in 2002), usually, it seems, on Sunday afternoons, when the museum is at its most packed.

The Richelieu Wing houses works from Flanders, Holland/The Netherlands, Germany and France (14th to 17th centuries), while the second floor of Sully is devoted to French paintings of the 17th, 18th and 19th centuries.

Break for Lunch

At this point, you'll probably be firmly in need of refreshment. Options in the vicinity of the Louvre are numerous; six recommendations are given in the 🍽 box *(see right)*.

THE TUILERIES

Once sated, head directly west of the pyramid for a stroll round the **Jardin des Tuileries ❷** (rue de Rivoli, 1st; daily 7.30am–7pm; free). Once a rubbish tip and clay quarry for tiles (*tuiles*, hence the name), the garden was created in 1564 for Catherine de Médicis in front of what was then the Palais des Tuileries *(see p.34)*. The Italian-style garden was intended to remind her of her native Tuscany.

Public Park

In 1664, Louis XIV's landscape gardener, André Le Nôtre, redesigned the park with his predilection for straight lines and clipped trees. It was opened to the public and became the first fashionable outdoor area in which to see and be seen, prompting the addition of the first deckchairs and public toilets.

In the 1990s the gardens were renovated, reinstating Le Nôtre's original design and incorporating a new sloping terrace and enclosed garden.

Food and Drink 🍽

④ CHEZ LA VIEILLE – ADRIENNE
1 rue Bailleul, 1st; tel: 01 42 60 15 78; €€€
Classic bistro with good food in homely portions. The even more classic (Corsican) owner will eulogise about his tripe and *pot-au-feu*, then talk at length on his various desserts.

⑤ LA FERME OPÉRA
55–7 rue St-Roch, 1st; tel: 01 40 20 12 12; €€
Self-service deli with healthy salads, sandwiches, fruit juices, cakes and tarts. Good-quality ingredients.

⑥ LE RUBIS
10 rue du Marché-St-Honoré, 1st; tel: 01 42 61 03 34; €
Wine bar with rustic *plats du jour* such as sausages with lentils. Food is served at lunch only, but the bar functions from noon until 10.30pm.

⑦ L'ARDOISE
28 rue du Mont Thabor, 1st; tel: 01 42 96 28 18; closed Sun lunch and Mon; €€
Excellent food from chef Pierre Jay. Unlike many bistros it opens on Sunday evening.

⑧ LE POQUELIN
17 rue Molière, 1st; tel: 01 42 96 22 19; €€€
Next to the Comédie-Française theatre and named after the playwright Molière (his real name was Poquelin), this institution offers bourgeois comfort and reliable food. Good *prix-fixe* menu.

⑨ BAR DE L'ENTR'ACTE
47 rue de Montpensier, 1st; tel: 01 42 97 57 76; €
In an otherwise chic area, just round the back of the Palais-Royal theatre, this bar has shabby appeal. Serves simple snacks throughout the day.

Other Museums
In a separate wing of the Louvre (entrance at 107 rue de Rivoli, www.lesartsdecoratifs.fr; Tue–Fri 11am–6pm, Sat–Sun 10am–6pm; charge) are three other collections, covering the decorative arts, fashion and textiles, and advertising. The Musée des Arts Décoratifs presents a survey of interior design from medieval tapestries to 21st-century design. The Musée des Arts de la Mode et du Textile covers Paris fashions and textiles from the 16th century to the present, and the Musée de la Publicité exhibits advertising paraphernalia from the Middle Ages to the present day.

Above from left:
soaking up some rays
in the Tuileries;
sculpture by Aristide
Maillol; contemplating
Monet's *Waterlilies
(Nymphéas)* in the
Musée de l'Orangerie;
Jeu de Paume.

The Passerelle Solférino, a footbridge across the Seine opened in 1999, links the southwestern corner of the gardens to the Left Bank.

Arc de Triomphe du Carrousel

Approaching the gardens from the Louvre, you pass through the **Arc de Triomphe du Carrousel ❸**, which is the smallest of the three arches on the Royal Axis (the others being the Arc de Triomphe and the Grande Arche at La Défense; *see also p.30*). Erected in 1808 by Napoleon to commemorate his Austrian victories, the pink arch is a rather garish imitation of the triumphal arches built by the Romans, and the four galloping horses on top are copies of four gilded bronze horses, stolen by Napoleon from St Mark's Square in Venice to decorate this memorial. After the emperor's downfall in 1815, the originals were returned.

Sculpture Garden

In front of the arch, where the Tuileries Palace once stood, is a group of sculptures of sensuous nudes, created between 1900 and 1938 by Aristide Maillol to adorn the ornamental pools. Numerous other sculptures decorate the gardens, including works by Marly, Le Paultre and Coustou, who were among the first artists to work in the Louvre after Louis XIV abandoned it for Versailles. There are also works by much later artists, including Rodin, Jean Dubuffet, Ellsworth Kelly and David Smith.

Hexagonal Pool

At this point continue westwards along the Terrasse du Bord de l'Eau, where Napoleon's children played under the watchful gaze of their father, to the **hexagonal pool** – still a favourite spot for children with boats. There are usually plenty of chairs around here, if you are in need of a rest and even a snooze.

THE ORANGERIE

In the southwest corner of the Tuileries is the **Musée de l'Orangerie ❹** (tel: 01 44 77 80 07; www.musee-orangerie.fr; Wed–Mon 9am–6pm; charge).

The Lost Tuileries Palace

In between the Louvre and the Tuileries Garden was once another palace. Originally built by Catherine de Médicis in the 1560s, it was later occupied by Louis XIV while he waited for Versailles to be built. In the Revolution, however, Louis XVI and Marie Antoinette were forced back to the Tuileries from Versailles and held under house arrest there. The palace was stormed and looted by the mob, leaving over 1,000 corpses strewn around the complex; the king and queen took refuge with the Legislative Assembly. The palace was attacked twice more by revolutionaries, in 1830 and 1848, only to be restored, and then finally burned in 1871 during the Paris Commune, as a symbol of the former royal and imperial regimes.

Waterlilies

The building was constructed as a hot-house by Napoleon III, but since the 1920s has been the showcase for eight massive canvases of waterlilies, *Les Nymphéas*, by Claude Monet. In these works, the Impressionist painter captured the play of light and colour on the pond in his garden at Giverny *(see p.96)* at different times of day, and in doing so caught a dream-like feeling of infinite space. Extensively renovated and reopened in 2006, the two elegant oval rooms upstairs display the paintings as originally prescribed by Monet himself.

Basement Gallery

In the gallery space downstairs is the **Jean Walter and Paul Guillaume Collection**, with high-quality examples of the work of Cézanne, Renoir, Matisse, Picasso, Soutine, Modigliani, Utrillo, Henri Rousseau and others.

JEU DE PAUME

With place de la Concorde on your left, walk to the **Jeu de Paume** ❺, in the northwest corner of the Tuileries. The building was originally constructed in 1861 to house real-tennis courts (hence the name, which means real tennis in French), though it soon became an art museum.

Centre National de la Photographie

The building now houses the stylish **Centre National de la Photographie** (tel: 01 47 03 12 50; www.jeudepaume. org; Tue noon–9pm, Wed–Fri noon– 7pm, Sat and Sun 10am–7pm; www. jeudepaume.org; charge), which puts on exhibitions of all photographic disciplines, including major fashion retrospectives and contemporary video installations. The Centre has another building, in the Marais, *see p.54*.

Resistance Effort

From 1940 to 1944 the Jeu de Paume was used to store artworks stolen from French Jews by the Nazi regime. The museum's curator, Rose Valland, a member of the Resistance, secretly recorded details of the 20,000 artworks that came through the depot on their way to Germany. She even notified her fellow *résistants* about which trains contained France's art treasures, so they would not blow them up. The 1964 John Frankenheimer film *The Train* was based on her experiences.

Below: at the Musée de l'Orangerie.

THE 7TH

The 7th arrondissement has some of the city's grandest monuments set amongst wide avenues, lofty mansions, ministries and embassies. Most impressive of all is that most iconic of Parisian – and French – symbols: the Eiffel Tower.

DISTANCE 4.5km (2¾ miles)
TIME A full day
START Tour Eiffel (Eiffel Tower)
END Musée d'Orsay
POINTS TO NOTE

Consider doing this tour on a Thursday, when the Musée d'Orsay (at the end of the route) has a late closing time of 9.45pm. At the start of the route, expect queues at the Eiffel Tower, which is always busy.

Whichever direction you approach it from, you can't miss the **Tour Eiffel ❶** (Eiffel Tower; Champs de Mars; tel: 01 44 11 23 23; www.tour-eiffel.fr; daily Sept–mid-June 9.30am–11.45pm for lifts, 9.30am–6.30pm steps only, mid-June–Aug 9am–12.45am for lifts and steps, last lift 45 min before closing; charge). At 300m (985ft), the tower is still the city's tallest structure, though no longer the world's tallest – an honour held until 1930, when New York's Chrysler Building surpassed it by 19m (62ft).

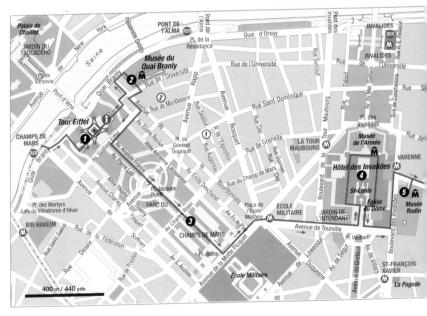

History

The tower was built according to plans by architect Gustave Eiffel between 28 January 1887 and 31 March 1889 for the Paris Universal Exhibition of 1889 and was intended to stand for only 20 years. Initially, the reception to the tower was frosty, with the Opéra architect Charles Garnier and the novelist Guy de Maupassant among its most vocal opponents. Maupassant organised a protest picnic under the tower's legs: 'the only place out of sight of the wretched construction'.

But the advent of radio and the tower's usefulness as a site for antennae secured its future. Even so, it survived a lightning strike in 1902, being 'sold' twice for scrap by a con artist in 1925, a demolition order from Hitler as the Allies neared Paris in 1944, and the ravages of corrosion: tons of rust were removed during its 100th birthday face-lift.

First and Second Platforms

The first platform is 57m (187ft) up, while the second level is at 115m (377ft). In total, there are 1,652 steps. The standard way to ascend is either on foot or in the glass-walled elevators, for which there are always long queues. As you ascend, bear in mind that in the past the tower's more foolhardy visitors have climbed up the outside and run, cycled or ridden motorbikes up and down the steps.

One way of avoiding the queues is to go for a meal at the Jules Verne restaurant, on the second platform (booking essential on tel: 01 45 55 61 44), for which there is a private elevator. You pay a premium for this, but the views are unbeatable.

Third Platform

From the second platform, the only way up is by elevator, which means further queuing. This takes visitors to the third level, 300m (985ft) up, from which there are views for approximately 65km (40 miles) on a clear day. The platform on the third level is glazed, and there are signs indicating which sights are which. Also on this level is Gustave Eiffel's salon, modelled as it would have been in his day, and the rather more recent addition of a gift shop.

Although the tower has restaurants, our recommendations are in the nearby streets below: **Café Constant**, see ❶①, and **Au Bon Accueil**, see ❶② *(p.39)*.

Above from far left: aspects of the tower; mini souvenirs.

Maintenance

Since it was built, the tower has been repainted 19 times. Each time, 60 tonnes of paint are required, plus 50km (31 miles) of security cords, 2ha (5 acres) of protective netting, 1,500 brushes and around 18 months to finish the task. In fact, the paint shades change from dark at the top to light at the bottom, so that the eye perceives the tower as being one uniform colour (the sky being light and the ground being dark).

Above from left:
at the Musée du Quai
Branly; interior view of
the dome of the
Église des Invalides;
Rodin's *The Thinker*;
admiring the art at the
Musée d'Orsay.

Bonaparte's Tomb
Napoleon died in
1821 on the island of
St Helena. In 1840,
after seven years of
negotiation between
the British and Louis-
Philippe, King of
France, the coffin was
exhumed and then
opened for two
minutes before being
transported to France
aboard the frigate
La Belle Poule.
Reputedly, the
body was perfectly
preserved. The tomb
you see today
consists of six layers
of coffins within a
sarcophagus of
Russian red porphyry.

QUAI BRANLY

After lunch, you may wish to see the city's newest museum, the **Musée du Quai Branly ❷** (37 quai Branly; tel: 01 56 61 70 00; www.quaibranly.fr; Tue, Wed, Sun 11am–7pm, Thur–Sat 11am–9pm; charge). To reach it, head east from the Eiffel Tower. The anthropology museum opens a window on to cultures as diverse as those of the Pacific Islands and Africa.

CHAMPS DE MARS

Now returning to the Eiffel Tower, walk up through the **Champs de Mars ❸**. Once a military parade ground for drilling 10,000 men, it stretches away from the river, ironically, via the glass Wall for Peace, up to the **École Militaire**, France's officer-training academy. Napoleon famously graduated from here in just one year instead of two. Turn left on avenue de la Motte Picquet to place de l'École Militaire, then take the 45-degree turn on to avenue de Tourville, where the **Hôtel des Invalides ❹** is on your left at place Vauban.

LES INVALIDES

The building of a home and hospital for aged and wounded soldiers was initiated by Louis XIV in 1670 using Libéral Bruant, and later Hardouin Mansart, as architects. It once housed 6,000 invalids. Now, part is still a hospital; the rest a museum of military history.

There is also a chapel for the veterans, who were once required to attend daily, and a separate royal chapel, the **Église du Dôme** (129 rue de Grenelle, 7th; tel: 08 10 11 33 99; www.invalides.org; daily Oct–Apr Mon–Sat 10am–5pm, Sun 10am–5.30pm, May–Sept Mon–Sat 10am–6pm, Sun 10am–6.30pm, also Apr–Sept Tue until 9pm, July–Aug dome open until 6.45pm; closed first Sun of month; charge), with a gilded dome. Since 1840 the latter has been dedicated to the worship of Napoleon.

The **Musée de l'Armée** (details same as for the Église du Dôme above; charge) comprises the royal armoury (from which, in 1789, revolutionaries commandeered 30,000 rifles for storming the Bastille), a fine collection of paintings (note Ingres' *Emperor Napoleon on the Throne*), and sections on the two world wars.

MUSÉE RODIN

As you leave Les Invalides turn left on boulevard des Invalides, cross over and then turn right at rue de Varenne. On your right is the **Musée Rodin ❺** (79 rue de Varenne; tel: 01 44 18 61 10; www.musee-rodin.fr; Tue–Sun 10am–5.45pm, winter till 4.45pm; charge).

The museum is housed in the Hôtel de Biron, built in 1728 as a private residence for a wig-maker who had got lucky on the stock market. Rodin moved here in 1908 and struck a deal with the government to bequeath all his works to the state on condition that they would be exhibited in the house and park.

Highlights

As you approach the house, you will find Rodin's famous statue, *The Thinker*, set high up amongst the greenery. Once inside, the decor is bare but elegant: wooden floors, a marble staircase, gilt mirrors, French windows, fine ceilings. As well as Rodin's works on display here, there are also paintings by Van Gogh, Monet and Renoir, and sculptures by Camille Claudel, Rodin's assistant and mistress. The difficulties of the creative life were multiplied for her as a woman, and she finished all but forgotten in a mental institution. The beautiful gardens behind the house are populated with more of Rodin's statues, and there is also a café.

MUSÉE D'ORSAY

Continue down rue de Varenne, past **L'Arpège**, see ⑪③, an excellent consideration for lunch or dinner, then turn left at rue de Bellechasse. If you overshoot the turning, on your right on rue de Varenne is the **Hôtel Matignon**, the residence of the French prime minister. Following rue de Bellechasse to the river, you come to the **Musée d'Orsay** ❻ (1 rue de la Légion d'Honneur; quai Anatole France; tel: 01 40 49 48 14; www.musee-orsay.fr; Tue–Sun 9.30am–6pm, Thur till 9.45pm; charge).

This art museum was originally a railway station, built for the Universal Exhibition of 1900. It was subsequently used as a prisoner of war depot during World War II, a set for several films, and then an auction house, before finally becoming a museum in the 1980s.

Exhibits

Dedicated to art from 1848 to 1914, the galleries are organised roughly chronologically. On the ground floor, where trains from southwest France once puffed in, you are taken from Delacroix and Corot up to the birth of Impressionism with early Monet and Renoir. On the mezzanine floor are sections on Art Nouveau design, paintings by Vuillard and Bonnard, and sculpture by Maillol and Rodin. There is also a restaurant with an exuberant Belle Epoque interior and an iconic clock. On the top level, which is often crowded, are the Post-Impressionists, notably Van Gogh, Cézanne, Seurat, Toulouse-Lautrec and Degas.

Ending the route here, note that a good restaurant for dinner is just beyond the museum (due east), see ⑪④.

La Pagode

The next road south from rue de Varenne is rue de Babylone, where at 57bis is La Pagode cinema (tel: 01 45 55 48 48). The building is a gorgeous 19th-century copy of a Japanese pagoda with a wonderfully lavish, gilded interior and a pretty, overgrown garden.

Food and Drink

① LE CAFÉ CONSTANT
139 rue St-Dominique, 7th; tel: 01 47 53 73 34; Tue–Sun; €€
At this traditional café-bistro, with a zinc bar and blackboard menu, chef Christian Constant does high-quality cooking at good prices.

② AU BON ACCUEIL
14 rue de Monttessuy, 7th; tel: 01 47 05 46 11; Mon–Fri; €€€
The decor here is sophisticated and elegant, with a lightness of touch; likewise the cooking. The *prix-fixe* dinner menu (around €30) is exceptional value. Sit on the terrace for views of the Eiffel Tower.

③ L'ARPÈGE
84 rue de Varenne, 7th; tel: 01 47 05 09 06; Mon–Fri; €€€
Chef Alain Passard has been called 'the poet of *terroir*' for his imaginative menus and signature dessert of tomato *confite* with 12 seasonings (if you can name them, the dish is free).

④ LE VOLTAIRE
27 quai Voltaire, 7th; tel: 01 42 61 17 49; Tue–Sat; €€
The food at this riverside bistro runs the whole gamut from rustic (such as sautéed rabbit) to luxury (lobster omelette).

CHAMPS-ÉLYSÉES AND GRANDS BOULEVARDS

This route covers some of the city's smartest avenues, squares and shops, and some big, bold attractions: from the monumental Arc de Triomphe to the Belle Epoque Grand and Petit Palais, and the capital's historic department stores.

Above: smart jewellers; *grand magasin.*

DISTANCE 4.75km (3 miles)

TIME A full day

START Arc de Triomphe

END Palais Royal

POINTS TO NOTE

This is a fairly long route, so consider taking the green no. 73 bus down the Champs-Élysées after visiting the Arc de Triomphe to conserve your energy for the second half of the tour. Book in advance for the Grand Palais, if you want to avoid the queues.

There is a lot to take in on this route, so you might consider doing it in two halves: the Arc de Triomphe to place de la Concorde, and the Madeleine to the Palais Royal.

ARC DE TRIOMPHE

At metro Charles-de-Gaulle-Étoile, take the subway to access the centre of the roundabout, amidst a chaotic whirl of cars (prangs here are specifically excluded from most insurance policies). In the middle is the **Arc de**

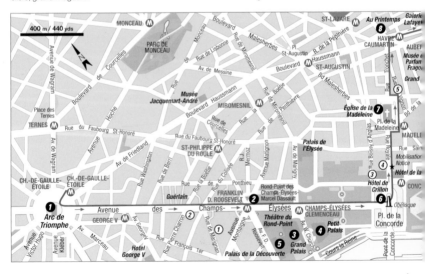

Triomphe ❶ (place Charles-de-Gaulle; tel: 01 55 37 73 77; www.arc-de-triomphe.monuments-nationaux.fr; daily Apr–Sept 10am–11pm, Oct–Mar 10am–10.30pm; lift for disabled visitors; charge), begun by Napoleon in 1806 but not completed until 30 years later under King Louis Philippe.

It commemorates Napoleon's army and is decorated with reliefs of famous victories. On the right (with your back to the Champs-Élysées) is the *Marseillaise*, sculpted by François Rude and representing 'Nation' leading the French into combat for the country's freedom. Under the arch is the **Tomb of the Unknown Soldier**, sited here in 1920 and with a flame of remembrance kept constantly alight.

From the top of the monument you can enjoy a spectacular view of the 12 avenues that radiate from l'Étoile (meaning 'of the star'), as the square is generally known. It was the 'other' Napoleon (Bonaparte's nephew, known to some as 'Napoleon the Little'), who, together with the Prefect of Paris, Baron Haussmann, created these wide boulevards flanked by chestnut trees.

CHAMPS-ÉLYSÉES

First initiated by Louis XVI in 1667, the **Champs-Élysées**, or 'Elysian Fields' were laid out by landscape architect André Le Nôtre as an extension of the Jardin des Tuileries, running west from the Louvre. During the Second Empire (1852–70) the avenue gave way to sumptuous hotels, chic shops and desirable corporate addresses. In 1871, Bismark's Prussian troops marched up here in triumph, and in 1940 Hitler's did likewise. Today, however, the avenue is home to cinemas, restaurants and the swanky flagship stores of large chains.

Above from far left: view from the Arc de Triomphe; underneath the arch.

Baron Haussmann Most of the boulevards and avenues on this route are the work of Baron Georges-Eugène Haussmann (1809–91), Prefect of Paris and town planner, who, with his network of wide tree-lined avenues, brought better health and light to the city, while also making it far more difficult for the post-Revolutionary mob to barricade the streets.

Left: Grand Palais.

Haute Couture

The first right turn off the Rond-Point is avenue Montaigne, where many leading fashion houses, including Céline, Chanel, Christian Dior, Loewe, Prada, Jil Sander, Ungaro and Louis Vuitton, have flagship stores.

Between the top end of the avenue and the **Rond-Point ❷** at the halfway stage, you pass the high-class **Hotel George V** on the avenue of the same name on your right and the Guérlain perfume store, with its opulent interior, on your left at no. 68.

After the Rond-Point, on your right (before the Grand and Petit Palais) is the **Théâtre du Rond-Point**, with its stylish interior (and bar). Meanwhile, on your left is the **Palais de l'Élysée**, the president's residence, down avenue de Marigny. If lunch is already a consideration at this stage, a chic choice is **Spoon**, see ⑪①; **Ladurée**, see ⑪②, is worth a visit at any time of day.

GRAND AND PETIT PALAIS

The Grand and Petit Palais, on avenue Winston Churchill, were built for the World Fair in 1900. The **Grand Palais ❸** (3 avenue du Général Eisenhower, 8th; tel: 01 44 13 17 17 for information, 08 92 70 08 40 for bookings; www.rmn.fr; daily except Tue 10am–8pm,

Below: macaroons at Ladurée.

Wed until 10pm; charge), with its 5,000 sq m (54,000 sq ft) of space, hosts blockbuster art exhibitions and the annual Paris Motor Show.

The Rococo-style **Petit Palais ❹** (avenue Winston Churchill, 8th; tel: 01 53 43 40 00; www.petitpalais.paris.fr; daily except Mon 10am–6pm, Thur until 8pm for special exhibitions; charge) houses the collection of the **Musée des Beaux-Arts de la Ville de Paris**. The building, inspired by the Grand Trianon at Versailles *(see p.92)*, with its polychrome marble, magnificent long gallery and arcaded garden, houses the municipal fine and decorative arts collection, including Greek and Roman antiquities, icons, paintings and Art Nouveau furniture.

PALAIS DE LA DÉCOUVERTE

Behind the Grand Palais on avenue Franklin D. Roosevelt is the **Palais de la Découverte ❺** (tel: 01 56 43 20 20; www.palais-decouverte.fr; Tue–Sat 9.30am–6pm, Sun 10am–7pm; charge), a science museum that is particularly fun for children. It is arranged as a series of interactive experiments, with highlights including a planetarium, electrostatics room and an area explaining acoustics.

PLACE DE LE CONCORDE

Now proceeding to the bottom of the Champs-Élysées, you enter **place de la Concorde ❻**, flanked by copies of Guillaume Coustou's *Marly Horses* (the originals are in the Louvre, *see pp.29 and 31*). In the centre of this

grand square is an **obelisk** from the tomb of Ramses III in Luxor. It was a gift from the Viceroy of Egypt in 1829 and took four years to get here. Previously, this spot had been occupied by the guillotine, and it was here that Louis XVI was beheaded in January 1793. His last words were: 'May my blood bring happiness to France.'

On the west side of the square is the **Jardin des Tuileries** *(see p.33)*, whereas on the north side are two identical palaces, designed in 1753 by Louis XV's architect, Ange-Jacques Gabriel. The right-hand one houses the naval ministry; the other is the **Hôtel de Crillon** *(see p.110)*, see ⑪③. The latter was where Marie Antoinette came for piano lessons, where the American delegation to the Paris Peace Conference stayed in 1919, and where the German high command ensconced itself in World War II.

Walk up rue Royale between the two palaces. On the wall of no. 4 is an oddity: a mobilisation notice, now framed, from the start of World War I. On the other side of the road is **Maxim's**, see ⑪④, which is good for an extravagant lunch.

THE MADELEINE

Before long, rue Royale opens out into **place de la Madeleine**, dominated by the neoclassical **Église de la Madeleine** ❼ (tel: 01 44 51 69 00; www.eglise-la madeleine.com; daily 9am–7pm; free). The church is the fruit of 80 years of anguished debate and false starts – the site was mooted for a stock exchange, public ballroom, library and railway sta-

tion – until 1806, when Napoleon ordered that a temple to his army be built by Barthélemy Vignon. It took until 1842 for it to be finished, by which time it was decided to consecrate it as a church. Today, it is noted for having one of the finest pipe organs in the city (the composers Saint-Saëns and Fauré were both organists here).

Food and Drink

① SPOON, FOOD & WINE
12 rue de Marignan, 8th; tel: 01 40 76 34 44; closed Sat; €€€€
The prototype of chef Alain Ducasse's global kitchens, which mix and match cuisines from around the world. Food is imaginative and precisely executed, though not cheap (try the less expensive lunch menu). Americana desserts include bubble-gum ice cream. The interior is perhaps over-designed, with the white wall-coverings at lunchtimes being raised in the evening to reveal purple upholstered walls. Book ahead.

② LADURÉE
75 Champs-Élysées, 8th; tel: 01 40 75 08 75; daily 7.30am–11pm; €€–€€€
The Parisian 'laboratory' of master macaroon-makers Ladurée employs around 45 pâtissiers, who produce tiptop macaroons every day and develop new flavours such as rose petal or liquorice. At this Champs-Élysées branch you can also enjoy breakfast or a full meal of French classics at the restaurant amid Louis XIV-style decor. Other branches include 16 rue Royale (also on this walk).

③ BAR DU CRILLON
6 rue Boissy d'Anglas, 8th; tel: 01 44 71 15 39; daily 11am–2am; €€€
Top hotel with a restaurant and bar where Ernest Hemingway drank when he had the money. The turn-of-the-20th-century decor has been given a designer face-lift by Sonia Rykiel. No jeans or trainers.

④ MAXIM'S
3 rue Royale, 8th; tel: 01 42 65 27 94; closed Sat lunch, Sun and Mon; €€€€
Founded by its namesake as a tiny bistro, Maxim's is now an Art Nouveau *restaurant de luxe*, owned by fashion designer Pierre Cardin and serving grand dishes in an old-fashioned way. Upstairs a museum 're-creates' the rooms of a rich courtesan using Cardin's Art Nouveau collection.

Above from left:
elegant Musée Jacquemart-André; velvet seats at the Palais Garnier; place Vendôme at dusk.

Jacquemart-André

Take a slight detour off our route, to 158 boulevard Haussmann and the Musée Jacquemart-André (tel: 01 45 62 11 59; www.musee-jacquemart-andre.com; daily 10am–6pm; charge). The museum houses a collection of art and furniture that once belonged to wealthy collector Edouard André and his wife, erstwhile portrait painter, Nélie Jacquemart. Highlights include works by Boucher, Rembrandt and Titian, as well as a wonderfully sumptuous dining room (11.45am–5.30pm) with a trompe l'oeil ceiling by Tiepolo, vast windows and delicious cakes.

Outside, the square offers a flower market as well as the main branches of France's best-known delicatessens, **Fauchon** and **Hédiard**, and the showroom of **Maille**, the mustard makers.

Beyond the Madeleine, walk up rue Tronchet passing the turning on your right for rue Vignon and **Le Roi du Pot-au-Feu**, see ⑪⑤, on the way.

GRANDS BOULEVARDS

Turn right on to boulevard Haussmann, home to the city's most famous department stores, **Au Printemps** ❽ at no. 64, and, nearby at no. 40, **Galeries Lafayette** ❾, both as noteworthy for their architecture as their vast stock.

At place Diaghilev turn right down rue Scribe. On this road are the 1862 **Grand Hotel** and the **Musée de la Parfumerie Fragonard** (9 rue Scribe; tel: 01 47 42 04 56; www.fragonard.com; Mon–Sat 9am–6pm, Sun except in winter 9.30am–4.30pm; free), which focuses on the art of perfume-making.

OPÉRA

Now turn left on to rue Auber to arrive at place de l'Opéra, where the **Palais Garnier** ❿ (tel: 08 92 89 90 90; www.operadeparis.fr; daily 10am–6pm; charge) puts on opera and ballet alongside the newer Opéra Bastille *(see p.55)*. It takes its name from its architect, Charles Garnier, who in 1860 was commissioned by Napoleon III to build an opera house reflecting the pomp and opulence of the Second Empire. The auditorium, decked out in velvet and

gilt, is dominated by a vast chandelier, which once crashed down on the audience in 1896. The ceiling was painted by Marc Chagall in 1964. A visit also takes in a library and museum, displaying scores, costumes and sets.

PLACE VENDÔME

As you leave place de l'Opéra, take rue de la Paix, which leads southwest at the bottom of the square. Its exclusive jewellers give a hint as to why it is the most expensive street in the French version of the Monopoly board game.

At its end, you reach the elegant **place Vendôme** ⓫. The square's centrepiece was originally an equestrian statue of Louis XIV, erected in 1699. This was destroyed during the Revolution and then replaced by Napoleon with the **Colonne de la Grande Armée**, modelled on Trajan's Column in Rome and made from 1,250 cannons captured from the Austrians and Russians. This in turn was pulled down during the 1871 Commune, only to be rebuilt later.

All the same, the square has in fact survived revolution and insurrection remarkably well. Today it is home to wealthy bankers, the salons of leading dress designers, top-price jewellers and the Hotel Ritz *(see p.112)*, where Princess Diana spent her last evening before her fateful car journey in 1997.

ST-ROCH

At the southern end of place Vendôme, turn left on to rue St-Honoré. Before long, on your left at no. 296, is the late

Baroque church of **St-Roch** ⓬ (tel: 01 42 44 13 20; daily 9am–7pm; free). Begun in the 1650s by architect Jacques Lemercier, who also worked on the Louvre, it contains the funerary monuments of landscape designer André Le Nôtre, the playwright Corneille and encyclopedist Diderot. On the church's exterior are pockmarks from musket shot after Napoleon's troops put down a Royalist revolt here in 1795.

COMÉDIE-FRANÇAISE

Now continue to place André Malraux, home to the French national theatre, the **Comédie-Française** ⓭ (entrance on place Colette; tel: 08 25 10 16 80; www.comedie-francaise.fr). Most productions are of the classical repertoire, by playwrights including Molière, Racine and Corneille.

PALAIS ROYAL

On the far side of the theatre is the **Palais Royal** ⓮. The palace's main courtyard, which is entered through the archway, contains 250 black-and-white striped columns, erected by artist Daniel Buren in 1986. Beyond are elegant gardens (daily dawn–dusk; free) enclosed by a three-storey peristyle erected in 1780 to house cafés, shops and apartments, and, with its rents, to replenish the coffers of its owners, the Orléans family, after a century of profligate spending. The passageways are enjoying a regeneration sparked by the opening of fashion designer Marc Jacobs' flagship store here.

Built for Cardinal Richelieu, and subsequently the childhood home of Louis XIV, the palace passed into the hands of the dukes of Orléans in the early 1700s. They turned it into a den of gambling and prostitution and forbade the police entrance. It was a focal point for intrigue during the Revolution, and afterwards, once restored to the Orléans, as iniquitous as before. Wellington supposedly lost so much money in its casinos that Parisians claimed they had recouped the cost of their war reparations. Today, it is a tamer place, housing the Ministry of Culture and Constitutional Council.

At this, the route's end, you can rejoin the metro just south of the Palais Royal or, to the north, visit **Willi's Wine Bar**, see ⑪⑥, for a drink.

Shopping Arcades
Slip out of the northern end of the Palais Royal's gardens and cross the tiny rue des Petits Champs. To your left are Galerie Vivienne (pictured) and Galerie Colbert, beautifully preserved skylit passages with mosaic floors and brass lamps, and both lined with shops full of curiosities.

Food and Drink 🍴

⑤ LE ROI DU POT-AU-FEU
34 rue Vignon, 9th; tel: 01 47 42 37 10; closed Sun and mid-July–mid-Aug; €
Traditional bistro (think red-and-white checked tablecloths) specialising in *pot-au-feu*. Once a rural stew eaten by peasant farmers, it is now a fashionable dish among Parisian gourmets. The best part is the bone marrow. Other French classics are also well executed here.

⑥ WILLI'S WINE BAR
13 rue des Petits Champs, 1st; tel: 01 42 61 05 09; closed Sun; €€
Chef François Yon's combination of the day's fresh produce and inspiring cooking is compelling. Add to this a lengthy wine list and the prime location, and the reasonable prices seem almost miraculous.

5 BEAUBOURG AND LES HALLES

This compact area is really in the thick of things, historically, artistically and commercially. Whereas once the city's food markets drew the crowds, today, the attractions are modern art, historic monuments and upmarket food shops.

DISTANCE 2.5km (1½ miles)
TIME Half a day
START Rue Rambuteau
END Rue de Rivoli
POINTS TO NOTE

Allow at least a couple of hours in the Centre Pompidou – longer, if you are particularly keen on modern and contemporary art. The time above allows for the former, plus a stop for breakfast and lunch at each end of the tour.

Food and Drink 🍴

① LE PETIT MARCEL

65 rue Rambuteau, 4th; tel: 01 48 87 10 20; cash only; €€
Inside, the walls are lined with Art Nouveau tiles and the ceiling is painted; outside, there is seating on the terrace. The menu comprises standard French fare – salads, steak frites, omelettes, tarts – but all well prepared, inexpensive and tasty.

Jazz Venues
On rue des Lombards, near the church of St-Merri, are three of Paris's most famous jazz clubs: Le Baiser Salé, Le Duc des Lombards and the Sunset/Sunside.

Beginning on rue Rambuteau and fortified with strong coffee from **Le Petit Marcel**, see 🍴①, walk round to the front of the Centre Pompidou, where the sloping cobbled terrace acts as a stage for fire-eaters, mime artists, hairbraiders and musicians.

CENTRE POMPIDOU

The **Centre Pompidou** ❶ (place Georges Pompidou; tel: 01 44 78 12 33; www.centrepompidou.fr; Wed–Mon 11am–9pm; tickets until 8pm; charge except for EU citizens under 26), or 'Beaubourg,' as it is known locally, after the street that runs behind it, continues where the Musée d'Orsay *(see p.39)* leaves off, with art from 1905 onwards.

The Architecture

The building was completed in 1977 to designs by architects Renzo Piano and Richard Rogers. The museum is now so popular (some years attracting more visitors than the Louvre) that it is hard to appreciate the initial storm of criticism regarding its 'inside-out' architecture (blue units transport air conditioning, green ones are water circulation, red tubes are transport routes and yellow ones indicate electric circuits). However, it suffered extensive weathering and corrosion and required a major renovation in the late 1990s.

Entrance and Services

Inside, on the ground floor, there is a complete posting of the centre's events and exhibits. There is often a free exhi-

bition in the massive entrance hall itself, while on the mezzanine level there is a post office, internet café and a shop selling a selection of works by modern designers. On the first floor there is a public library and a cinema.

The Permanent Collection

A selection from the permanent art collection of 60,000 works is on levels 4 and 5. Parts are rehung every year. The period from 1905 to the 1960s is dealt with on level 5, with works by artists such as Kandinsky, Klee, Klein, Matisse, Picasso and Pollock, and sections on Dadaism and Surrealism. Art from the 1960s to the present day is on level 4 and includes works by Andy Warhol, Verner Panton, Joseph Beuys, Jean Dubuffet and Anselm Kiefer.

Studio Brancusi and IRCAM

In front of the Pompidou is a pavilion containing the studio (Wed–Mon 2–6pm; included in main ticket) of Romanian-born sculptor, Constantin Brancusi (1876–1957). The artist lived in this studio for 30 years, bequeathing it to the French state on his death. It has been set up here just as he left it.

Next to the Pompidou, and part of the same organisation, is the Institute of Research and Co-ordination into Acoustics and Music (IRCAM), on place Igor Stravinsky. This centre, created by composer Pierre Boulez, hosts concerts of avant-garde music.

ST-MERRI

Beyond the Stravinsky Fountain (see right), on the south side of the square is the Gothic church of **St-Merri** ❷ (76 rue de la Verrerie; tel: 01 42 71 93 93; www.saintmerri.org; Mon–Sat 3–7pm; free). It dates mostly from the 16th century, but its bell has been tolling since 1331, which makes it the oldest in Paris. The organ was once played by the composer Camille Saint-Saëns.

Above from far left:
Centre Pompidou with its 'inside-out' architecture.

Stravinsky Fountain
Between the Centre Pompidou and the church of St-Merri is a colourful fountain with grotesque creatures and contraptions spouting water. It was created by artists Niki de Saint-Phalle and Jean Tinguely as a homage to composer Igor Stravinsky's *Firebird* ballet.

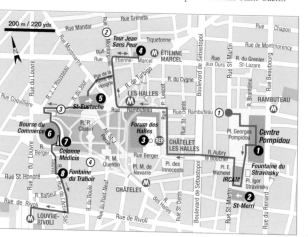

Golden Snails

Among the bakeries, fishmongers and greengrocers of rue Montorgueil, look out for the restaurant L'Escargot at no. 38 with wonderful gold snails on its sign *(see right)* and a painted ceiling (taken from actress Sarah Bernhardt's manor house) in the entrance hall.

Above: fresh fish and squash at rue Montorgueil market and the excellent kitchen store E. Dehillerin.

RED LIGHTS

Exiting the church on rue St-Martin, turn right, up towards the Pompidou, and then left at rue Aubry le Boucher. Go straight on, across the busy boulevard de Sébastopol and on to rue Berger. At the corner of rue St-Denis, take a good look up and down. Rue St-Denis is the city's main red-light district. The area in which you stand is fairly tame, though things become more overt a little further along.

LES HALLES

Rue Berger now opens out into place Joachim du Bellay. The Fontaine des Innocents, the Renaissance fountain in the middle, was moved here from the nearby Cimetière des Innocents, which was demolished in 1786 after flesh-eating rats started gnawing into people's houses.

Leaving the place by rue Pierre Lescot on your right, you come to **Les Halles ❸**. The name refers to the covered food market that was established here by King Philippe Auguste in 1183. In the 1850s, huge glass-and-iron buildings were erected, and Emile Zola later wrote a novel, *The Belly of Paris* (1873), set around the area. Sadly, in 1971 the structure was demolished in the interests of safety and urban renewal, and the markets moved to the southern suburb of Rungis. Today, the site is occupied by a widely disliked multi-level shopping centre, although regeneration on and around the complex has started.

TOUR JEAN SANS PEUR

Past Les Halles, turn left on to rue Rambuteau and right on to rue Montorgueil. Where rue Étienne-Marcel crosses rue Montorgueil, turn right for the **Tour Jean Sans Peur ❹** (20 rue Étienne-Marcel; tel: 01 40 26 20 28; www.tourjeansanspeur.com; mid-Apr–mid-Nov Wed–Sun 1.30–6pm, mid-Nov–mid Apr Wed, Sat–Sun 1.30–6pm; charge), a fortified town house built 1409–11 by Jean, Duke of Burgundy.

The duke acquired his nickname, meaning 'John the Fearless', from military exploits in Bulgaria against the Turks. On return to Paris, he assassinated his rival, Louis d'Orléans, and sparked the Hundred Years' War between the Armagnac and Burgundian factions *(see p.52)*. Jean fled, but returned two years later and, necessarily security conscious, added the tower to his mansion. In the end he was assassinated (by an axe blow to the head) at a meeting with the future Charles VII.

ST-EUSTACHE

Retracing your way back down rue Montorgueil, perhaps stopping en route at **Stohrer**, see ⑪②, take the narrow passage de la Reine de Hongrie on your right, then continue over to the Impasse St-Eustache, which leads to the church of **St-Eustache ❺** (2 impasse St-Eustache; tel: 01 42 36 31 05; www.saint-eustache.org; Mon–Fri 9.30am–7pm, Sat 10am–7pm, Sun 9am–7pm; free). Built from 1532 to 1640, it has a Gothic exterior and fine Renaissance

interior. Its 8,000-pipe organ is highly renowned: Berlioz and Liszt played here in the 19th century, and recitals are still held weekly, at 5.30pm on Sundays.

Around Place René Cassin

Emerging from the other (south) side of the church, you find yourself on place René Cassin with its massive sculpture by Henri de Miller of a giant head and cupped hand, entitled *Écoute* (Listen). Continue west on rue Coquillière. A curiosity on your right is **E. Dehillerin**, purveyors of pots and pans to Paris's chefs. Also here is the renowned brasserie **Au Pied de Cochon**, see ⑪③.

BOURSE DE COMMERCE

The rotunda on your left is the **Bourse de Commerce** ❻ (2 rue de Viarmes; tel: 01 55 65 55 65; Mon–Fri 9am–6pm; free access to main hall; charge for tours, which are for parties with advance booking only). The Bourse was built in 1767 on the site of Marie de Médicis' palace, and functioned as the city's grain market. Today, it houses the Chamber of Commerce. The original wooden dome was replaced by an iron structure in 1809, before being covered in copper, and then glass. Inside are frescoes evoking the history of trade between the continents.

ASTROLOGER'S COLUMN

As you leave the Bourse, turn left and go round the back to find the **Colonne Médicis** ❼. The plaque at its base states that the pillar is the sole relic of the

manor house constructed in 1572 by Catherine de Médicis (wife of Henri II). She had a 31m (102ft) -high tower built for her astrologer, Cosimo Ruggieri, who, with his patron, regularly climbed up the spiral staircase within to read the future in the stars. The chamber at the top was once entirely glazed, but only the metal skeleton remains. Unfortunately, you can no longer go inside.

FONTAINE DU TRAHOIR

If lunch or dinner is now an urgent priority, head for the nearby **La Tour de Montlhéry**, see ⑪④. Otherwise, go down rue Sauval, turn left at rue St-Honoré and then immediately right on to rue de l'Arbre-Sec. On the street corner is the **Fontaine du Trahoir** ❽, a fountain rebuilt by Soufflot in 1776 and dripping with stone icicles. Follow the road to rue de Rivoli and turn right to rejoin the metro at Louvre-Rivoli.

La Galcante
At no. 52 rue de l'Arbre Sec is the Hôtel de Truden, built in 1717 for a wealthy wine merchant. In the courtyard is La Galcante, which sells historic newspapers, magazines and other printed ephemera.

MARAIS AND BASTILLE

Among the most vibrant areas of town, the Marais and the Bastille are an unlikely but successful blend of ingredients: aristocratic mansions, the centre of the gay scene, the home of the Jewish community, and a throbbing nightlife.

DISTANCE 4.5km (2¾ miles)
TIME A full day
START Hôtel de Ville
END Place de la Bastille
POINTS TO NOTE

It is not intended that you visit every museum. There is, however, the opportunity to combine a stroll in the historic streets with some shopping, lunch, a museum tour and finally a rest in a park or café.

The area covered in the first part of this tour was once a swamp - '*marais*' is French for 'marsh'. It was drained in the 16th century and developed as an aristocratic residential district, until, with the rise of Versailles, it fell into neglect. Largely untouched by town planner Baron Haussmann in the 19th century, it fell into further decline, until by the 1960s it was derelict and rat infested. Due to be cleared, it was saved by Culture Minister André Malraux, who safeguarded many of the buildings and

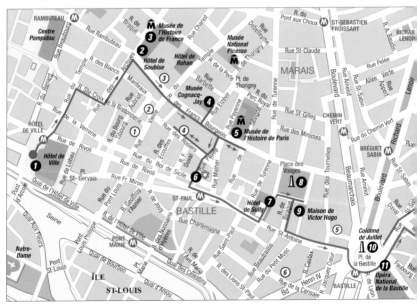

initiated the restoration. Today it is a fashionable quarter full of boutiques, galleries, bars and restaurants.

HÔTEL DE VILLE

Begin at the **Hôtel de Ville ❶** (29 rue de Rivoli; tel: 01 42 76 40 40; www.paris.fr; Mon–Sat 10am–7pm; charge), since 1357 the seat of local government in Paris. The building is a re-creation of the original structure, commissioned by François I in 1533 and gutted by fire during the Paris Commune of 1871.

It has been the scene of many historical events, including the proclamation of the Third Republic in 1870 and Charles de Gaulle's famous speech to the assembled crowds on 25 August 1944 during the Liberation of Paris.

Its most notable features are the extravagant Salle des Fêtes (ballroom), a magnificent staircase and some opulent chandeliers. On the north side, on rue de Rivoli, is an entrance to an exhibition with information about the city.

THE MARAIS

Head north from the pedestrianised square in front of the Hôtel de Ville, where, in medieval times, hangings and other gruesome executions took place. Cross the rue de Rivoli, walk up rue du Temple and turn right at rue Ste-Croix de la Bretonnerie, the centre of the gay scene. Turn left off this road on to rue des Archives and then continue until you reach rue des Francs-Bourgeois.

Hôtel de Soubise and Hôtel de Rohan
At no. 60, in the **Hôtel de Soubise ❷**, are the French National Archives, opened by Napoleon in 1808 and housing documents from the Merovingians to 1958. Napoleon III later opened the **Musée de l'Histoire de France ❸** (tel: 01 40 27 62 18; www.archivesnationales.culture.gouv.fr; Mon, Wed–Fri 10am–12.30pm, 2–5.30pm, Sat–Sun 2–5.45pm; charge) in the **Hôtel de Rohan** round the corner at 87 rue Vieille du Temple; this showcases the more prestigious documents.

If for nothing else, it is worth a visit for the magnificent buildings themselves, which were home to the Guise family from 1553; it is probably from here that the Catholic League planned the St Bartholemew's Day Massacre. In 1700, the Duke de Rohan, Prince of

Above from far left: boutique fashions at Manoush; crême-brulée at Georget; place des Vosges.

Pawnbroker
Across the road from the National Archives, behind an austere facade, is the Crédit Municipal, the state pawnbroker. Nicknamed *ma tante* ('my aunt'), the lending facility was opened in 1777, and you can still obtain cash on the value of objects surrendered to its charge.

Sunday Shopping

The Marais is one of the few Paris districts in which a large number of shops open for business on a Sunday, its busiest and most crowded day of the week.

Murder Scene

Just off rue des Francs-Bourgeois, opposite rue des Hospitalières St-Gervais, is the Impasse Arbalétriers. Here, in 1407, Charles VI's brother, Louis d'Orléans, was assassinated on the orders of Jean Sans Peur *(see p.48)*, thus sparking the Hundred Years' War. The path, now a dead end, once led to a field where crossbowmen used to practise, hence the name 'Arbalétriers'.

Soubise, bought the estate and revamped it, with Rococo interiors decorated by Boucher, Lemoine and van Loo.

Lunch Options and Shopping

While on rue Vieille du Temple, there are several good options for lunch,

---

Food and Drink 🍴

① LE PETIT FER À CHEVAL

30 rue Vieille du Temple, 4th; tel: 01 42 72 47 47; daily till 2am; €€
Cramped but fun café-bistro with a horseshoe-shaped bar out front and small box of a dining room with old metro benches at the back. A case study in artful insouciance.

② GEORGET

64 rue Vieille du Temple, 4th; tel: 01 42 78 55 89; Mon–Fri lunch and dinner, Sat dinner only; €€
Also known as Robert et Louise, this cosy restaurant with its roaring fire is a carnivore's delight: superb black pudding (accompanied by a lonely lettuce leaf), steak served on a wooden platter and thick, tasty beef stew.

③ LE DÔME DU MARAIS

53bis rue des Francs-Bourgeois, 4th; tel: 01 42 74 54 17; closed Tue lunch, Sun and Mon; €€€
Unstuffy restaurant in a grand setting (once the auction house for the state-owned pawnbrokers). Beautifully executed cooking in a modern style.

④ L'AS DU FALLAFEL

34 rue des Rosiers, 4th; tel: 01 48 87 63 60; closed Fri dinner and Sat; €
The place for fallafel. Try the special (vegetarian) sandwich: garlicky chickpea balls, hummous, fried aubergine, red cabbage, salted cucumber and harissa. Lamb chawarmas are also recommended. Hectic but fun ambience. Takeaway also available.

---

including **Le Petit Fer à Cheval**, see 🍴①, and **Georget**, see 🍴②. Back on rue des Francs-Bourgeois there are designer boutiques and cafés, too, notably **Le Dôme du Marais**, see 🍴③. When sated, continue a little further to find rue Elzévir on your left.

Musée Cognacq-Jay

The outside of the 1580s mansion at no. 8 rue Elzévir is understated, but inside is the exquisite fine and decorative art collection of Ernest Cognacq, who founded La Samaritaine department store in 1870, and his wife Marie-Louise Jay, in the **Musée Cognacq-Jay** ❹ (tel: 01 40 27 07 21; www.paris.fr; Tue–Sun 10am–6pm; free).

Here, 18th-century refinement is embodied in salons and 'cabinets' with the feel of a private house. On the panelled walls are paintings and drawings by Chardin, Nattier, Fragonard, Watteau, Reynolds, Guardi and Canaletto. Displayed on delicate furniture and in cabinets are Meissen porcelain figures by master modeller J.J. Kändler.

Musée National Picasso

While you're in this area, it's worth noting for future reference that just nearby is the **Musée National Picasso** (5 rue de Thorigny, tel: 01 42 71 25 21; www.musee-picasso.fr; closed for renovation until 2012). The museum is housed in the Hôtel Salé, so-called because its 17th-century owner grew rich through collecting taxes on salt. The paintings and other works of art in the collection were given to the state on the artist's death. Not all are by

Picasso: his personal collection includes works by Cézanne, Matisse (his great rival), Modigliani and Braque.

Hôtel Carnavalet

For now, though, the next stop is the **Musée de l'Histoire de Paris ❺** (Hôtel Carnavalet, 23 rue de Sévigné; tel: 01 44 59 58 58; www.carnavalet.paris.fr; Tue–Sun 10am–6pm; free). This is the city's historical museum, set within two adjoining 16th- to 17th-century mansions. In over 100 rooms, it tells the story of Paris from Roman times to the present using paintings, memorabilia and historic interiors.

The museum dates from 1866, when Baron Haussmann convinced the city to purchase many of the fine interiors of the aristocratic mansions he was then demolishing to make way for the new boulevards. These interiors were moved to the Carnavalet, one of Paris's first Renaissance buildings, and, fittingly, home from 1677 to 1696 to Madame de Sévigné, whose writings reveal so much about 17th-century aristocratic life.

Among the exhibits are the spinning wheel used by Marie Antoinette when in prison, as well as her son's tin soldiers (rooms 105–106); the chains used on one of the last prisoners at the Bastille (room 102); paintings of the prostitutes working the galleries of the Palais Royal (room 117); the Art Nouveau interiors of the Salon du Café de Paris and a jewellery shop from rue Royale (rooms 141 and 142); and Proust's cork-lined bedroom, in which he wrote much of his seven-volume masterpiece *À la recherche du temps perdu* (room 147).

Jewish Quarter

Leaving the Carnavalet, take rue Pavée opposite to reach the Jewish Quarter. Off to the right on rue des Rosiers are several Jewish bakeries and restaurants, including the excellent **L'As du Fallafel**, see ⑪④, a by-product, like many, of the Sephardic immigration after the French withdrawal from North Africa. Another café on the street, Jo Goldenberg's at no. 7, still bears the scars of a terrorist attack during the 1980s.

At 10 rue Pavée is the extraordinary **Synagogue ❻** (tel: 01 48 87 21 54; visits by request only; free). It is architecturally notable for its 1913 Art

Hammam
For a modern take on the traditional hammam, complete with steam room, massage and facial treatments, try Les Bains du Marais at 31–3 rue des Blancs-Manteaux (tel: 01 44 61 02 02; www.les bainsdumarais.fr). It also has a restaurant.

Nouveau facade by Hector Guimard, who also designed the furnishings inside. The building was severely damaged by a bomb (along with six other Parisian synagogues) during anti-Semitic demonstrations on the evening of Yom Kippur 1941. It was restored and is now a national monument.

Continue along rue Pavée and turn left on to rue de Rivoli, which soon becomes rue St-Antoine.

Food and Drink 🍴

⑤ BOFINGER
5–7 rue de la Bastille, 4th; tel: 01 42 72 87 82; daily noon–midnight; €€€
Paris's oldest brasserie, which served the city's first draught beer in 1864 when phylloxera struck France's vineyards. Spectacular Belle Epoque interior: a revolving door, a glass domed ceiling, squishy leather bench seats and, upstairs, wall paintings of kugelhof and pretzels. The menu offers several kinds of choucroute, seafood, pigs' trotters and Paris-Brest. Good wines, many available by the glass.

⑥ LE TEMPS DES CERISES
31 rue de la Cerisaie, 4th; tel: 01 42 72 08 63; Mon–Fri lunch only, closed Aug; no credit cards; €
Untouched by fashion or commercialism. Tasty, simple French food.

⑦ LE SOUK
1 rue Keller, 11th; tel: 01 49 29 05 08; Tue–Fri dinner only, Sat–Sun lunch and dinner; €€€
Excellent atmospheric Moroccan restaurant that serves up hearty, beautifully spiced cuisine. Choose from huge tagines, plentiful couscous plates and succulent lamb shanks followed by delicate pastries and end with a palate-cleansing mint tea.

Changing Fortunes
A sign of how things have changed around Bastille is to be found at 17 rue de la Roquette, just off rue St-Sabin. The bar La Rotonde is now a hang-out for the young and hip, but it was previously a brothel whose owner was shot dead by a blind accordion player.

Hôtel de Sully
At no. 62, enter the large wooden doors of the **Hôtel de Sully** ❼ (tel: 01 42 74 47 75; www.jeudepaume.org; Tue–Fri 12–7pm, Sat–Sun 10am–6pm; charge). This impressive 17th-century mansion, built to plans by architect Jean Androuet du Cerceau in 1625 and then bought in 1635 by Sully (Finance Minister under Henri IV), is a splendid second venue for changing exhibitions mounted by the Centre Nationale de la Photographie *(see p.35)*.

Walk through the cobbled courtyard, and on into the pristine gardens. Voltaire was beaten with clubs here by followers of the Count de Rohan after a slanging match between the two at the Comédie-Française *(see p.45)*.

Place des Vosges
A gate in the far corner provides an escape on to **place des Vosges** ❽. Built from 1605 to 1612 by Henri IV, this large, elegant square was originally called place Royale, but was renamed in tribute to the first French *département* (county) to pay its war taxes to the Republican government. Famous past residents have included Madame de Sévigné, salon hostess and letter writer, at no. 1bis (born here in 1626), poet Théophile Gautier and writer Alphonse Daudet at no. 8, and Cardinal Richelieu at no. 21.

Maison de Victor Hugo
Located in the southeast corner of the square, at no. 6, is the **Maison de Victor Hugo** ❾ (tel: 01 42 72 10 16; www. paris.fr; Tue–Sun 10am–6pm; free),

erstwhile home of the author of *Les Misérables* and *The Hunchback of Notre-Dame*. Hugo lived here from 1832 to 1848, until Napoleon III's coup d'état forced him, as a staunch republican, into 20 years of exile on Guernsey. Inside, you can see his rooms, some furnished with a few of his own pieces – he was an expert, though eccentric, carpenter – as well as a number of his drawings and first editions.

BASTILLE

Leaving place des Vosges and the Marais behind, walk down rue de Birague and turn left at rue St-Antoine. As you approach place de la Bastille, **Bofinger**, see ⑪⑤, a grand establishment for lunch or dinner, is off to your left on rue de la Bastille. Off to your right, down rue du Petit Musc, is rue de la Cerisaie, where 1,000 cherry trees once grew. This is now the location for the modest but charming **Le Temps des Cerises**, see ⑪⑥.

Place de la Bastille

The vast **place de la Bastille** ❿ takes its name from the notorious prison stormed by revolutionaries on 14 July 1789. On its capture, only seven prisoners remained inside, but the rebels did find it a useful supply of arms and gunpowder. The Banque de France office now stands on its site.

In the centre of the square is the **Colonne de Juillet** (July Column), which was erected in the 19th century to honour victims of the 1830 and 1848 revolutions. The golden statue at the top, the *Génie de la Bastille*, is a representation of Liberty.

Opéra National de la Bastille

On the southeast side is the **Opéra National de la Bastille** ⓫ (120 rue de Lyon; tel: 01 40 01 19 70; www.opera deparis.fr; charge for tours, cash only). One of Mitterrand's *grands projets (see p.30)*, it was constructed in 1989 to designs by Canadian-based Uruguayan Carlos Ott, but has since been plagued with criticism: for its acoustics, its vast cost and the poor quality of its architecture. Netting has already been put up to stop its granite slabs falling down.

The Fashionable East

If you take rue de la Roquette off place de la Bastille and turn right on to rue de Lappe, you find yourself on a street lined with bars, nightclubs, cafés and boutiques, a reflection of the area's fashionable status, which boomed in the 1990s. (Nowadays, it's still trendy, although not quite as cutting edge as it once was.) The area's fashion credentials are also reflected in its peppering with contemporary galleries. At the end of rue de Lappe, turn left on to rue de Charonne, where **Lavignes Bastille** ⓬ (est.1973), at no. 27, is one of the best-known galleries in the neighbourhood (Andy Warhol exhibited here). For more contemporary art, additional galleries can be found further up on your left on rue Keller, as well as a nice Moroccan restaurant, **Le Souk**, see ⑪⑦. To return to Bastille, retrace your steps or turn left at the northern end of rue Keller on to rue de la Roquette.

Skating Parisians

Each Friday night, except in wet weather, 15,000 Parisian rollerbladers gather at 10pm at place Raoul Dautry at the foot of the Tour Montparnasse in the 14th *arrondissement* for Pari Roller, a three-hour skating tour of the city. Less experienced bladers can take part in a skate organised by Rollers et Coquillages that leaves place de la Bastille at 2.30pm on Sundays. See www.pari-roller.com and www.rollers-coquillages.org.

THE LATIN QUARTER

This university area takes you from Roman remains to medieval theological colleges, to Enlightenment seats of learning, to the student riots of 1968. And the tradition continues today, with students and academics smoking outside the libraries, drinking in the cafés and browsing in the bookshops.

DISTANCE 3km (2 miles)
TIME A full day
START Jardin des Plantes
END Place St-Michel
POINT TO NOTE
The first part of the route is good for children, who should love the attractions of the Jardin des Plantes.

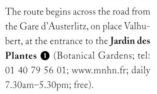

Ancient Trees
The Jardin des Plantes contains many trees planted as long ago as the early 18th century, including a Cretan maple planted in 1702, and a cedar (of 1734) brought from the Lebanon by the botanist Bernard de Jussieu in his hat, because he had broken the pot.

The route begins across the road from the Gare d'Austerlitz, on place Valhubert, at the entrance to the **Jardin des Plantes ❶** (Botanical Gardens; tel: 01 40 79 56 01; www.mnhn.fr; daily 7.30am–5.30pm; free).

JARDIN DES PLANTES

The gardens were established by Louis XIII's physician in 1626 as a source of medicinal herbs and opened to the public in 1640 as the 'Jardin du Roi'. In the 1700s, a maze, amphitheatre and several museums were added.

On your left as you enter is the first of these museums, that of palaeontology and comparative anatomy, the **Galerie de Paléontologie et d'anatomie comparée** (tel: 01 40 79 56 01; daily 10am–5pm; charge), displaying fossils, skeletons and shells. Outside are huge replica dinosaurs, including a nice stegosaurus.

Museum of Mineralogy and Geology
Now make your way to the statue of the zoologist Jean-Baptiste Lamarck (1744–1829), and from here walk all the way up the avenue of plane trees to the statue of an illustrious former keeper of the gardens, Georges-Louis Leclerc, Count de Buffon (1707–88), at the other end. En route, you pass the rose garden in front of the **Galerie de Minéralogie et de Géologie** (Museum of Mineralogy and Geology; tel. 01 40 79 56 01; daily 10am–6pm; charge), which contains meteorites, minerals, jewels and giant crystals.

The Zoo
Within the gardens, on the opposite side, is the **Ménagerie** (tel: 01 40 79 37 94; daily 9am–5pm; charge). This zoo was established during the Revolution with animals from royal and aristocratic collections. Nowadays, there are around 240 mammals, 500 birds and 130 reptiles here.

Food and Drink 🍴
① MOSQUÉE DE PARIS
39 rue Geoffroy-St-Hilaire,
5th; tel: 01 43 31 38 20; €
Within the mosque is a beautiful Moorish tearoom with a tiled interior and shady terrace.

Beyond the statue of de Buffon at the end of the avenue is the **Grande Galerie de l'Évolution** (tel: 01 40 79 54 79; www.mnhn.fr; Wed–Mon 10am–6pm; charge), opened in 1889 to display part of the collection of 7 million skeletons, insects, and stuffed birds and mammals. Most are now in an underground research centre, but the recently renovated exhibition space shows some 7,000 choice specimens, including 257 endangered or extinct species.

MOSQUÉE DE PARIS

Leaving the gardens by the gate on rue Geoffroy St-Hilaire, cross over towards the corner of rue Daubenton and the **Mosquée de Paris ❷** (Paris Mosque; 2bis place du Puits de l'Ermite; tel: 01 45 35 97 33; www.mosquee-de-paris. net; tours daily 9am–noon and 2–6pm; charge). This Hispano-Moorish-style complex was built in 1922 to commemorate North African participation in World War I. It incorporates a museum of Muslim art, a pretty tearoom, see ⑪①, and a Turkish bath.

ARÈNES DE LUTÈCE

Turn left out of the tearoom and continue walking north along rue Geoffroy St-Hilaire. Go straight on at the crossroads, as the road becomes rue Linné. Take a left into rue Arènes. On your right is the entrance to the **Arènes de Lutèce ❸** (daily 8am–5.30pm, till 10pm in summer; free). This Roman amphitheatre was rediscovered in the 1860s during the construction of the nearby rue Monge. Where gladiators once fought before an audience of 15,000, elderly men now play boules.

RUE MOUFFETARD

As you leave, turn right and climb the few steps to rue Rollin. At the end of this road, turn left on to rue du Car-

Old Horse Market
In 1900, there were over 80,000 horses in Paris, and the main market for them was at the southern end of rue Geoffroy St-Hilaire. All that is left today is the fine Louis XV building at no. 5, where the market authorities once had their headquarters, and the smart offices at nos 11–13. An inscription on the facade of the latter reads 'Dealers in thoroughbreds, ponies of all kinds and shire horses'.

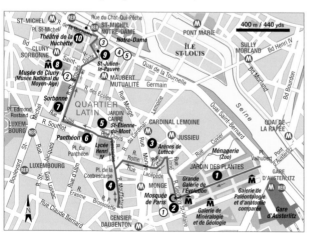

Panthéon Extras
In addition to the Panthéon's tombs, highlights include a 67m (220ft) replica of Foucault's pendulum (an experiment to show the rotation of the earth) and frescoes on the life of St Geneviève by Puvis de Chavannes.

dinal-Lemoine (Ernest Hemingway lived on this road, on the third floor of no. 74). You soon come to **place de la Contrescarpe**, with its pleasant cafés. In the 1530s Rabelais, Ronsard and du Bellay met at the Cabaret de la Pomme de Pin at no. 1.

On the far side of the square is **rue Mouffetard ❹**, a former Roman road, famous for its food market (Tue–Sat, all day, and Sun am). This now-desirable street was once part of a working-class neighbourhood; off to your right is rue du Pot-de-Fer, where writer George Orwell lived at no. 6 while researching *Down and Out in Paris and London*.

TOWARDS THE PANTHÉON

Retrace your steps to place de la Contrescarpe, then keep going, along rue Descartes, into the heart of the Latin Quarter. This university area derives its name from the fact that Latin was

widely spoken here in the Middle Ages. Turn left at rue Clovis, to see, on your left, the **Lycée Henri IV**, one of France's most elite secondary schools, and, on your right, the church of **St-Étienne-du-Mont ❺** (place Ste-Geneviève; tel: 01 43 54 11 79; Tue–Sun 10am–7pm; free). Inside the latter is the only Renaissance rood screen (1541) in Paris.

The Panthéon

Coming out into the vast place du Panthéon, the neoclassical **Panthéon ❻** (tel: 01 44 32 18 00; www.pantheon paris.com; daily 10am–6pm; charge) looms up before you. It was designed by Soufflot as a church to St Geneviève for Louis XV, who wanted to give thanks for his recovery from illness. After the Revolution it became a Temple to Reason and the burial place of the nation's great minds, including Voltaire, Rousseau, Hugo, Zola, and Pierre and Marie Curie.

THE SORBONNE

Next take rue Cujas off the square to your right, turn right on to rue St-Jacques and head down the hill. The **Sorbonne ❼**, one of the oldest colleges (1253) of the university of Paris, is on your left. The buildings date mainly from the late 19th century, although the domed chapel, in which Cardinal Richelieu is buried, is 17th century. At the bottom of the hill on your right is the Collège de France, founded in 1530 as a humanist alternative to the decidedly Catholic Sorbonne.

The Lady and the Unicorn

The Musée de Cluny's tapestry series *The Lady and the Unicorn* is one of the greatest works of art of the Middle Ages in Europe. It depicts the five senses plus a sixth, mysterious, sense.

In this last scene, the lady puts into her jewel-case the collar that she was wearing in the other five. Above her is the inscription, 'To My Only Desire'. The most popular theory is that this signifies the refusal of temptation, and the renunciation of the five senses, previously sated.

MUSÉE DE CLUNY

Turn left on to rue des Écoles, where **Le Balzar**, see ⑪②, is on your left. Turn right at the square Painlevé for the **Musée de Cluny – Musée National du Moyen Age ❽** (tel: 01 53 73 78 00; www.musee-moyenage.fr; Mon, Wed–Sun 9.15am–5.45pm; charge).

Once the residence of the Abbots of Cluny, this is the only surviving Gothic residence in Paris. It also incorporates the remains of a huge Gallo-Roman bathhouse complex, built *c.*200 AD by the guild of *nautes* (boatmen); ships' prows are carved on the arch supports of the frigidarium (cold-bath house).

On display in the main museum are medieval manuscripts, textiles (notably the *Lady and the Unicorn* tapestries – *see opposite*), stained glass and sculpture, including 21 of the original heads of the kings of Judah, crafted in 1220 for the front of Notre-Dame *(see p.26)* but vandalised in the Revolution.

TOWARDS THE SEINE

After the museum, return to rue St-Jacques and continue downhill, bearing right on to rue Dante. This street becomes rue du Fouarre, where, on your left, is the calm **La Fourmi Ailée**, see ⑪③. Good alternative eating options entail a detour to the right to rue des Grands-Degrés, see ⑪④ and ⑪⑤.

Square Viviani

A little further on is **square Viviani**, on the far side of which is the 12th-century church of **St-Julien-le-Pauvre ❾**. It

was originally a sanctuary for pilgrims on their way to Compostella, before becoming the university church; it is now used by the Greek Melkites.

Taking rue St-Julien towards the river you reach quirky English-language bookshop **Shakespeare & Co** (Mon–Sat 10am–11pm, Sun 11am–11pm), on the left. On the pavement by the river are *bouquinistes* (riverside bookstalls).

Rue de la Huchette

Walking west, cross rue St-Jacques and go down **rue de la Huchette**. There are tourist traps on this medieval street, but look out for **rue du Chat-Qui-Pêche**, the city's narrowest street on the right and the **Théâtre de la Huchette ❿** *(see right)* at no. 23. You emerge on place St-Michel with its **fountain** of St Michael slaying a dragon.

Above from far left: coffee in St-Germain; Panthéon; Shakespeare & Co.

Bald Soprano

The minuscule Théâtre de la Huchette (23 rue de la Huchette; tel: 01 43 26 38 99; www.theatre-huchette.com) has been playing Ionesco's *La Cantatrice Chauve* (The Bald Soprano) since 1957. It's a fun evening, if your French is up to it, although the theatre can get very hot in summer. Tickets are generally available on the day.

Food and Drink 🍴

② LE BALZAR
49 rue des Écoles, 5th; tel: 01 43 54 13 67; €€
Classic brasserie fare: snails, plaice in butter and veal's head with a mustardy *sauce ravigote* (Jacques Chirac's favourite). The waiters are consummate professionals in plunge-line waistcoats.

③ LA FOURMI AILÉE
8 rue du Fouarre, 5th; tel: 01 43 29 40 99; €
Ambient, inexpensive, haven of a tearoom-cum-restaurant that was formerly a women's library (the walls are still lined with books).

④ LE REMINET
3 rue des Grands-Degrés, 5th; tel: 01 44 07 04 24; daily for lunch and dinner; €€€
Chef Hugues Gournay's fine dishes include snails, whiting on aubergine caviar, and chestnut cake. Good-value lunch menu.

⑤ LES DEGRÉS DE NÔTRE DAME
10 rue des Grands-Degrés, 5th; tel: 01 55 42 88 88; €
Tasty menu of bistro fare and Morrocan cuisine. A bargain.

ST-GERMAIN

With its elegant streets and squares, St-Germain is a magnet for designer fashion shops, chic cafés and restaurants. But before the glossy present was a more rumbustious past: revolutionaries plotted, actors drank, and Hemingway stole pigeons from the Jardin du Luxembourg to cook and eat.

DISTANCE 3km (2 miles)
TIME A full day
START Place St-Michel
END Jardin du Luxembourg
POINTS TO NOTE
End your walk with a picnic in the Jardin du Luxembourg.

Below right:
a tempting display
of macaroons.

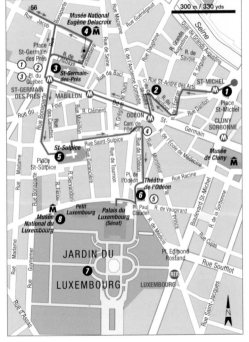

The route begins at **place St-Michel** ❶, from where you should head west on to rue St-André des Arts, into a warren of streets full of shops, bars and restaurants. Turn left on to rue de l'Éperon, right on to rue du Jardinet, then continue to cour de Rohan.

HISTORIC QUARTER

You finally emerge on to the **cour du Commerce St-André** ❷, where you should turn left. During the Revolution, Danton lived at no. 1 on this cobbled passage, Jean-Paul Marat had his printing works for the political newspaper *L'Ami du Peuple* (Friend of the People) at no. 8, and, in the courtyard of no. 9, Dr Guillotin was testing his gruesome invention on sheep.

Le Procope

On a tiny road parallel, look out for **Le Procope** (13 rue de l'Ancienne Comédie; tel: 01 40 46 79 00; 10.30am–1am), supposedly the oldest surviving café in Paris. It started out as a coffee house in 1686, and its success in those early days was owing to the performances of the Comédie-Française *(see p.45)* in a theatre nearby; the playwrights Racine and Molière were reportedly regular customers here.

BOULEVARD ST-GERMAIN

Exiting the passage, turn right on to boulevard St-Germain. You soon come to place St-Germain-des-Prés, where one of the city's oldest churches is situated, as well as a cluster of famous café-restaurants: the **Café de Flore**, **Les Deux Magots** and the **Brasserie Lipp**, see ①①, ② and ③.

St-Germain-des-Prés

The church of **St-Germain-des-Prés** ❸ (tel: 01 55 42 81 33; www.eglise-sgp.org; daily except Mon and Sat am 10.30am–noon and 2.30–6.45pm; free) takes its name from an 8th-century cardinal of Paris, who, on his death, was buried in the 6th-century abbey of Ste-Croix-St-Vincent on this site.

The present church was built in the 11th and 12th centuries and was once part of a vast monastery. During the Revolution, the monastery was suppressed, and 300 monks and priests were killed. The church survived and is the only Romanesque one left in Paris. Its troubles did not end there though: in the 19th century it was converted into a saltpetre factory and then underwent several less-than-sensitive restorations.

Inside, the 17th-century philosopher René Descartes' ashes are interred under the window in the second chapel. Outside, in square Laurent-Prache, are relics of a magnificent chapel built in 1255 by the architect of Sainte-Chapelle *(see p.25)*, Pierre de Montreuil, who was buried here. Look out also for Pablo Picasso's portrait bust of the poet Guillaume Apollinaire (1880–1918).

From the square, turn right on rue de l'Abbaye, then left on to the pretty rue de Furstemberg.

Above from far left: St-Germain-des-Prés; paying the bill; church of St-Germain; Brasserie Lipp.

Fashion Shopping
The streets south of boulevard St-Germain and around place St-Sulpice are lined with expensive clothes shops, including many designer names. Try, in particular, rue Bonaparte, rue du Four, rue du Dragon, rue de Grenelle and rue du Cherche-Midi.

Food and Drink 🍴

① CAFÉ DE FLORE
172 boulevard St-Germain, 6th; tel: 01 45 48 55 26; daily 7.30am–1.30am; €€€
Grand historic café with Art Deco interior of red seating, mahogany and mirrors. In the days when it was less expensive, it was frequented by Jean-Paul Sartre and Simone de Beauvoir.

② LES DEUX MAGOTS
6 place St-Germain-des-Prés, 6th; tel: 01 45 48 55 25; daily 7.30am–1am; €€€
Rival to Café de Flore, and also once habituated by Sartre and de Beauvoir, as well as Hemingway, Picasso and Gide, among others. Like many places that have become an institution, it is also now pretty expensive and can get very busy. Light food.

③ BRASSERIE LIPP
151 boulevard St-Germain, 6th; tel: 01 45 48 53 91; daily 9am–1am; €€€
Reportedly actress Emmanuelle Béart's favourite eatery and a good place to spot neighbourhood eccentrics. Brasserie classics.

MUSÉE DELACROIX

The **Musée National Eugène Delacroix** ❹ (tel: 01 44 41 86 50; www.musee-delacroix.fr; Mon, Wed–Sun 9.30am–5pm; charge), at nearby 6 place Furstemberg, comprises the 19th-century painter's former home, studio and garden. The artist moved here in 1857 to be near St-Sulpice *(see below)*, where he had been commissioned to paint several murals. He died in the bedroom in 1863. While the Louvre and Musée d'Orsay house his major Romantic paintings, here you can see smaller works and sketches.

TOWARDS ST-SULPICE

Back on rue de Furstemberg, continue as far as rue Jacob and turn left. At

Institut de France
Head north on rue Bonaparte instead of south, and on your right by the river is the Institut de France. The building houses the Académie Française, whose membership of 40 'immortels' are responsible for the official dictionary of the French language.

no. 56, peace documents recognising the independence of the US were signed by Benjamin Franklin and David Hartley, King George III's representative in France.

Retracing your steps, now turn right (south) down rue Bonaparte past a succession of stylish shops, including a branch of **Ladurée** *(see p.43)*, famous for its delicious macaroons. Eventually, you arrive at place St-Sulpice. This chic square is used every summer for an antiques fair and poetry fair. In the centre is the lion-flanked Fontaine des Quatre Évêques, built by Visconti in 1844 and showing four likenesses of bishops from the reign of Louis XIV.

ST SULPICE

The eastern side of place St-Sulpice is dominated by the vast Italianate church of **St-Sulpice** ❺ (tel: 01 42 34 59 98; www.paroisse-saint-sulpice-paris.org; daily 7.30am–7.30pm; free). Begun in 1646 to a design by Jean-Baptiste Servandoni, the church took a further five architects and 120 years to complete. The result is ponderous: the towers, one of which is higher than the other (unfinished), have been likened to 'municipal inkwells'. The church has many historical links, though: the Marquis de Sade was baptised here, Victor Hugo was married here, and it featured in Prévost's 18th-century novel *Manon Lescaut*.

Highlights
Inside, the first chapel on the right (Chapelle de Sainte Agnès) was decorated by Eugène Delacroix, and

Massacre of the Priests

In the Institut Catholique, at 74 rue de Vaugirard, is the chapel of St-Joseph-des-Carmes. As a result of a law of 17 August 1792, whereby all the monasteries had to be vacated, the Carmelite monastery here was converted into a prison for over 150 priests who had refused to take an oath to uphold the Constitution. As the Prussian army advanced, the prisoners were accused of spying for the enemy. After a mock trial, pikes, swords and makeshift weapons were used to kill 118 of the prisoners in the gardens near the steps (note the Latin inscription, 'hic ceciderunt', meaning 'here they fell'). Today, in the crypt, you can see the victims' remains – not a single skull is in one piece. On the upper floor in one of the former cells are traces of blood from the executioners' pikes.

completed two years before his death. In the nave are two great conch shells presented to François I by the Republic of Venice. Note also the fine organ with 6,700 pipes and check the noticeboard for details of concerts held in the church.

In the left wing of the transept is a gnomon, a white marble obelisk with a line of copper leading away from it in the floor, representing the Paris meridian. It was completed in 1727, and improved by Lemonnier in 1744. When the sun shines through the 'eye', located 25m (82ft) above the ground in a transept window facing south, the device is meant to indicate the 'true' midday hour and the approximate date.

ODÉON

Leaving the church, walk along rue St-Sulpice and turn left at rue de Condé to reach **carrefour de l'Odéon** (where an excellent lunch at **Le Comptoir**, see ⑪④, can be had). Next turn right up rue de l'Odéon, an enclave for publishers and antiquarian bookshops for at least 150 years. At no. 12 Sylvia Beach and the original Shakespeare & Co. bookshop *(see p.59)* first published James Joyce's *Ulysses*.

At the top of the road is the grand neoclassical **Théâtre de l'Odéon ⑥**, built from 1779 to 1782. It was here that Beaumarchais's *Marriage of Figaro* was first performed in 1784 and the actress Sarah Bernhardt gave many of her finest performances.

Beyond the theatre is rue de Vaugirard, where a pit stop at the engaging **Au Petit Suisse**, see ⑪⑤, may well be

required, before then finishing the route in the Jardin du Luxembourg.

JARDIN DU LUXEMBOURG

At the entrance to the **Jardin du Luxembourg ⑦** (daily dawn–dusk; free) is the **Palais du Luxembourg**, built in the 1620s for Marie de Médicis, widow of Henri IV, by Salomon de Brosse. Its Italianate style was supposed to remind Marie of the Pitti Palace in her native Florence. It now houses the Senate. Next door, at 19 rue de Vaugirard, is the **Musée National du Luxembourg ⑧** (tel: 01 42 34 25 95; www.museedu luxembourg.fr; Mon, Fri 10.30am–10pm, Tue–Thur 10.30am–7pm, Sat–Sun 9.30am–8pm; charge). Opened in 1750, it is France's oldest public art gallery and hosts major art exhibitions.

Inside the gardens are statues, fountains, a boating lake, lawns, cafés, a bandstand, a playground, sandpits, a theatre for marionettes, a merry-go-round, boules pitches, deckchairs, orchards with 300 varieties of apple, and an apiary, where you can take courses in beekeeping.

Above from far left: St-Germain street scene; detail from St-Sulpice; boules player; relaxing in the Jardin du Luxembourg.

Above: in the Jardin du Luxembourg.

Food and Drink 🍴

④ LE COMPTOIR
9 carrefour de l'Odéon, 6th; tel: 01 44 27 07 97; €€€
In the evenings, chef Yves Camdeborde's bistro offers a no-choice €40 meal that is so good you have to book months in advance. Lunchtime dishes are also tasty: iced cream of chicken soup and rolled saddle of lamb are typical.

⑤ AU PETIT SUISSE
16 rue de Vaugirard, 6th; tel: 01 43 26 03 81; €
Unpretentious café with terrace. Remains as it has been for decades. Snacks served noon till midnight.

MONTMARTRE

Romantic relic of a simpler, more vital world or clichéd victim of its own success? Approach Montmartre with a fresh mind and steer clear of the obvious tourist traps, and you will find plenty here to engage and surprise.

DISTANCE 3.5km (2¼ miles)
TIME A full day
START Les Abbesses
END Place de Clichy
POINTS TO NOTE

Montmartre's streets are very steep, so this is not the best route if you prefer easy walks on the flat. (Taking the funicular up the hill will take some strain out of the climb.) Make sure you wear comfortable flat shoes.

Montmartre has always stood slightly apart from the rest of the city. For much of the 19th century it was mined for gypsum and still retained a country charm with its vineyards, cornfields, flocks of sheep and 40 windmills. The lofty isolation of the hill and its cheap lodgings attracted artists and writers. Painters and their models frequented place Pigalle, and people flocked to the Moulin Rouge. Impressionism, Fauvism and Cubism were conceived in the area's garrets, bars and dance halls.

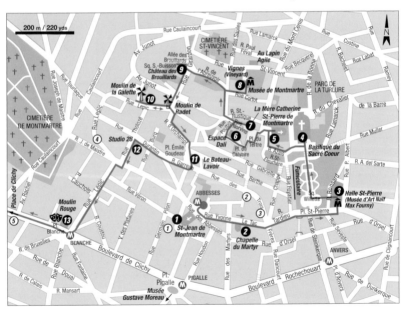

LES ABBESSES

At the exit of metro Les Abbesses, note the Art Nouveau canopy by Hector Guimard, one of only two (the other is at place Dauphine) in the city to survive. Opposite is another Art Nouveau structure: **St-Jean de Montmartre ❶**. Built 1897–1904 to designs by Anatole de Baudot, the church is an early example of construction with reinforced cement and brick. At first, many thought it would be unsafe, and demolition was imposed. Luckily, the relevant parties were eventually convinced.

Inside are several wall paintings (unfinished) executed at the end of World War I and depicting the Gospel of St-John. There is also fine glass, sculptural and mosaic decoration.

Now, making a mental note that nearby are a couple of good restaurants for later, see ⓘ❶ (from 7.15pm only) and ⓘ❷, head east off the square on rue Yvonne Le Tac. At no. 9 is the **Chapelle du Martyr ❷**, where, according to legend, St Denis, the first Bishop of Paris, picked up his head after being decapitated by the Romans in AD 287. He is then said to have walked off with it to where the basilica of St-Denis now stands 10km (6 miles) to the north. Montmartre means 'hill of the martyr'.

PLACE ST-PIERRE

The road now becomes rue Tardieu and then place St-Pierre. With Montmartre's white basilica rising above you, walk to the far side of the place, where, on your left, is the **Halle St-Pierre**. This 19th-century covered market hall designed by Victor Baltard (who designed the original Les Halles, *see p.48*) houses the **Musée d'Art Naïf Max Fourny ❸** (tel: 01 42 58 72 89; www.hallessaintpierre.org; daily 10am–6pm; charge), which shows brut and naïve artworks by artists from around the world. It also runs children's workshops, and has an excellent bookshop and café.

Now either walk up through square Willette, laid out in terraces in 1929, or take the funicular railway (the fare is one metro ticket) to reach the terrace in front of Sacré-Coeur.

SACRÉ-COEUR

Sacré-Coeur ❹ (35 rue Chevalier-de-la-Barre; tel: 01 53 41 89 00; www.sacre-coeur-montmartre.com; basilica: daily 6am–11pm, crypt and dome: summer 9am–7pm, winter 9am–6pm; entry to basilica free, charge for dome and crypt) was constructed after the

Breaking the Siege

It was from place St-Pierre that on 7 October 1870, Léon Gambetta, interior minister of the nascent Third Republic, took off in a yellow hot-air balloon to rally the army at Tours and relieve Paris from the Prussian siege.

Food and Drink

① CHEZ TOINETTE
20 rue Germain-Pilon, 18th; tel: 01 42 54 44 36; Mon–Sat from 7.15pm; €€€
Where many places in this part of town fob off unwitting tourists with overpriced fare, this amiable bistro has a good, well-priced blackboard menu that runs to steaks, wild-boar terrine, a lovely warm goat's cheese salad and prunes soaked in Armagnac.

② AU GRAIN DE FOLIE
24 rue de la Vieuville, 18th; tel: 01 42 58 15 57; €
A self-styled 'vegetarian place for non-vegetarians', this is a quaint spot for a healthy bite. Sit among the cooking implements and pot plants and enjoy a bowl of homemade soup, a crispy vegetable platter or a slice of savoury tart. The restaurant is a tight squeeze but that all adds to the friendly atmosphere.

Above from left:
wine bottles; artist's palette; museum sign.
Below: the vineyard.

Erik Satie

The composer Erik Satie (1866–1925) lived in various lodgings on rue Cortot in the 1890s, and conducted an affair here with the artist Suzanne Valadon, who lived a few doors away. You can visit the tiny bedroom at no. 6 (tel: 01 42 78 15 18; visits by appointment; free), which he referred to as his 'placard' (cupboard). On display are manuscripts, an engraving by Picasso, and sketches for the ballet, *Parade*.

suppression of the 1871 Paris Commune, which had been passionately supported by the anarchist Montmartrois. The church was built in appeasement for the bloodshed, and because of this, and its arguably rather mediocre architecture, has never been well-loved by local residents. To this day, it is often mocked in cabaret songs on the hilltop (known locally as La Butte).

Work started on the basilica in 1875 and was not completed until 1914, and it was then not consecrated until 1919. The architect, Paul Abadie, based his design on the Romano-Byzantine cathedral of St-Front in Périgueux and used Château-Landon stone, which secretes calcite when it rains, bleaching the walls a bone-white colour.

The dome, up 237 narrow spiral steps, offers a wonderful view over Paris. There is also a huge bell, the Savoyarde, weighing 18 tonnes. From the stained-glass gallery beneath is a good view of the cavernous interior.

PLACE DU TERTRE

Now head west from the church on rue Azais and turn right on to rue St-Eleuthère to arrive at place du Tertre, which regrettably now has more than its fair share of overpriced restaurants and bad would-be artists. Stay briefly on the square, however, for a couple of more worthwhile sights.

St-Pierre de Montmartre

On your right is the simple church of **St-Pierre de Montmartre** ❺ (tel: 01 46 06 57 63; daily 8.30am–7pm; free), the second oldest in Paris (after St-Germain-des-Prés), dating from 1133, and all that remains of the old Abbey of Montmartre. A Benedictine nunnery since the 12th century, the abbey was destroyed during the Revolution, and the last mother superior was guillotined at the age of 82, despite her deafness and blindness. The church itself was then abandoned and only

reconsecrated in 1908. It is noteworthy too that, according to the earliest biography of St-Ignatius Loyola, it was here that the vows were taken that led to the founding of the Jesuits.

Inside, the walls and columns (Roman in origin) of the nave seem to have bent with age and lean outwards. If you are here on Toussaint (All Saints' Day – 1 November), visit the small, romantic graveyard behind the church, since this is the only day of the year that it is open.

Dalí Museum

On the opposite side of the square is place du Calvaire, which forms a terrace with a fine view over Paris. At its far end, on the corner of rue Poulbot, is **Espace Dalí ❻** (11 rue Poulbot; tel: 01 42 64 40 10; www.daliparis.com; daily 10am–6pm; charge), with more than 300 works by the Surrealist artist.

The Original Bistro

Following rue Poulbot round, turn right at rue Norvins to reach 6 place du Tertre, home of **La Mère Catherine ❼**, reputedly Paris's first bistro. Originally a drinking den for revolutionaries (where Danton said 'eat, drink, for tomorrow we shall die'), the old inn apparently served Russian soldiers during the Allied occupation of 1814. As they ordered their drinks – forbidden by the Russian military authorities – they shouted 'bistro' meaning 'quickly', thereby creating a Parisian institution.

Leaving the crowd of place du Tertre behind, head back to rue Norvins, then off onto rue des Saules and take the second right on to rue Cortot.

MUSÉE DE MONTMARTRE

At 12 rue Cortot, in the oldest house on the Butte, is the **Musée de Montmartre ❽** (tel: 01 49 25 89 37; www.museedemontmartre.fr; Tue–Sun 11am–6pm, July–Aug Fri–Sun till 7pm; charge), which chronicles the life and times of the artists' quarter.

This manor house was originally the country home of Rosimund, an actor in Molière's theatre company who, in 1686, suffered the same fate his master had done 13 years earlier: he collapsed during a performance of *Le Malade Imaginaire*. Two hundred years later and the house had been divided into studios, with Renoir, Dufy, and Utrillo and his mother, Suzanne Valadon, living and working here *(see margin opposite)*.

The Displays

Today, the lower floors are devoted to the history of Montmartre through revolutions and wars, whereas the upper floors evoke the bohemian artistic life of legend. As well as a reconstruction of Utrillo's favourite café, L'Abreuvoir, there is an artist's studio and artworks by Utrillo, Dufy and Toulouse-Lautrec.

VINEYARD

Behind the museum (there are good views from its windows) are vineyards that were planted in 1933 in homage to the vines cultivated here since the Middle Ages. In early October, the grape harvest attracts hundreds of volunteers, and processions and parties take place in the neighbouring streets. About

Legendary Cabaret
Further down rue des Saules at no. 22 is Au Lapin Agile (tel: 01 46 06 85 87; www.au-lapin-agile.com; Tue–Sun 9pm–2am; charge). On wooden benches by scarred tables (though with original paintings by Gill and Léger), you are treated to a glass of cherries in *eau de vie* and a night of songs and poems in the tradition of Aristide Bruant. Once upon a time Renoir and Verlaine laid tables here, and Picasso paid for a day's meals with one of his *Harlequin* paintings: now worth millions of pounds.

Above from left:
ball skills at the Sacré-Coeur; boules on square Suzanne-Buisson; the Moulin Rouge; Pigalle, downhill from Montmartre.

Van Gogh's Home
No. 54 on the old quarry road of rue Lepic was home to Vincent Van Gogh and his brother Theo, an art dealer for two years in the late 1880s. During that time, Van Gogh showed his paintings at Le Tambourin, a seedy cabaret on boulevard de Clichy, until the owner demanded he remove them, as they upset her customers.

300 litres (634 pints) of wine are sold at auction, with proceeds going to the Montmartre Festival Committee.

CASTLE OF THE MISTS

On the other side of rue des Saules from rue Cortot is rue de l'Abreuvoir, which becomes the allée des Brouillards. Here, **square Suzanne-Buisson** occupies the former gardens of the **Château des Brouillards ❾**, which stands opposite. The house was built in 1772 and takes its name from the windmill that was here before and could only be seen when the fog lifted. Converted outhouses in its grounds were once inhabited by Renoir and the Symbolist poet Gérard de Nerval (who hanged himself in 1855, leaving a note saying, 'Don't wait for me, for the night

will be black and white'). Later the château became a dance hall, and then a squat before being restored.

RENOIR'S WINDMILL

Turn south on rue Girardon, then right on to rue Lepic. On your right is the **Moulin de la Galette ❿**. Built in 1604, the windmill became a dance hall in the 19th century and was immortalised by Renoir in his 1866 painting of the same name. Earlier, in the 1814 siege of Paris, the four Debray brothers fought to save their windmill from the Russians; one of them was subsequently crucified on its sails. Today, the windmill is better protected, as a notice proclaims: 'Residence under electronic, radar and guard-dog surveillance'.

BATEAU-LAVOIR

Now go back to rue Girardon, noting the other windmill here, the Moulin de Radet. Head south along the narrow rue d'Orchampt and continue to its end and place Émile Goudeau. At no. 13, recently built artists' studios stand in place of the wooden ramshackle building in which Braque and Picasso invented Cubism. **Le Bateau-Lavoir ⓫**, so named because it resembled a floating laundry, was where Picasso painted *Les Demoiselles d'Avignon* (1907), recalling the prostitutes of Barcelona; in rooms alongside, Apollinaire and Max Jacob developed their liberated verse-form. Sadly, the building burnt down in 1970 just as it was about to be renovated.

The New Athens

In the mid-19th century, the area south of boulevard de Clichy now known as La Nouvelle Athènes (New Athens) attracted writers, artists, composers, actresses and courtesans. For a sniff of this rarefied past, visit the Musée Gustave Moreau (14 rue de La Rochefoucauld; tel: 01 48 74 38 50; www.musee-moreau.fr; Wed–Mon 10am–12.45pm, 2–5.15pm; charge) with its lovely double-height studio packed with Symbolist paintings, or the Musée de la Vie Romantique (*right*) at 16 rue Chaptal (tel: 01 55 31 95 67; Tue–Sun 10am–6pm; charge) with its memorabilia on the novelist George Sand and her circle of friends, including her lover the composer Chopin.

STUDIO 28

Now, if you are in need of a pit stop, turn left on to rue des Trois Frères to find the bistro, **L'Annexe**, see ⑪③. Otherwise, to continue the route turn right on to rue Garreau, which soon becomes rue Durantin, and, at the crossroads with rue Tholozé, turn left.

L'Age d'Or

On your left is the famous cinema, **Studio 28** ⑫, where, in 1930, Luis Buñuel's *L'Age d'Or* (The Golden Age) caused a riot on only its second screening due to its overtly sexual content (the film only got past its censors through its being excused as 'the dream of a mad man'). Members of the fascist League of Patriots threw ink at the screen, attacked members of the audience, and destroyed art work by Dalí, Miró, Man Ray, Yves Tanguy and others on display in the lobby. The film was subsequently banned for 50 years.

Rue Lepic

At the end of rue Tholozé, turn right, and soon after join the lower reaches of rue Lepic. At no. 42 is **À la Pomponette**, see ⑪④, while at no. 15 is **Les Deux Moulins**, where Amélie Poulain waited on tables in the eponymous film. At the bottom of rue Lepic, turn right on to boulevard de Clichy.

THE MOULIN ROUGE

Almost immediately on your right is the **Moulin Rouge** ⑬ (82 boulevard de Clichy; tel: 01 53 09 82 82; www.

moulinrouge.fr; charge), where a troupe of scantily clad 'Doriss' dancers delight spectators with their nightly show.

The club's history is gloriously scandalous. In 1896, the annual Paris Art School Ball was held here and featured the first fully nude striptease, by one of the school's models. She was arrested and imprisoned, and students went to the barricades in the Latin Quarter, proclaiming 'the battle for artistic nudity'; two students died in the scuffles with police.

Sparing a thought for the poet Jacques Prévert, who used to live just next door, now continue down the boulevard de Clichy towards place de Clichy, where the **Wepler**, see ⑪⑤, an old-world brasserie, forms a fitting end to this tour.

Food and Drink 🍴

③ L'ANNEXE

13 rue des Trois Frères, 18th; tel: 01 46 06 12 48; Mon–Sat; €€
Cosy place run by an elderly couple who offer homely French cooking with a Swiss accent.

④ À LA POMPONETTE

42 rue Lepic, 18th; tel: 01 46 06 08 36; Mon dinner only, Tue–Sat lunch and dinner; €€€
Family-run bistro offering excellent renditions of classic French dishes.

⑤ WEPLER

14 place de Clichy, 18th; tel: 01 45 22 53 24; daily noon–1am; €€€
Once a restaurant with a sideline as a billiards hall, now a brasserie with an emphasis on seafood. Indulge in a huge platter of oysters, whelks, clams, langoustines, crab and sea urchins.

Pigalle

At the bottom of the Butte is Pigalle, or 'Pig Alley', as it was known to American soldiers during World War II. Once known exclusively for being the city's seedy red-light district, the area is cleaning up its act and is in parts now edgily cool. Some sex shops and seedy nightspots are still in evidence, but many of the old brothels and erotic cabarets are being replaced by trendy clubs (such as the Divan du Monde at 75 rue des Martyrs), chic boutiques and fashionable bars and restaurants. Look out at 8 rue Navarin for the hip Hôtel Amour (tel: 01 48 78 31 80; www.hotelamour.com; see p.113), which plays on the district's erotic past.

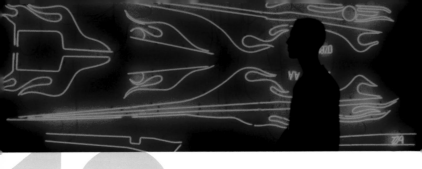

TROCADÉRO

This walk to the Trocadéro in the 16th offers a varied selection of Parisian museums. Art or fashion, Asian antiquities or naval history: choose carefully which ones to visit, since to see them all would be exhausting.

DISTANCE 1.25km (¾ mile)
TIME Half a day
START Place de l'Alma
END Palais de Chaillot
POINTS TO NOTE
The time above includes the walk and a stop in two of the museums listed.

Flame of Liberty
At place de l'Alma, look out for la Flamme, a counterpart to the flame of the Statue of Liberty (gifted to the US by France). The monument was a focus for tributes to Princess Diana, whose fateful car accident occurred in the underpass just below.

Start at place de l'Alma *(see left)*, then head west up avenue du Président Wilson to the first of the museums on this route. On your left, at 13 avenue du Président Wilson, is the **Palais de Tokyo ❶**, built, along with the nearby Palais de Chaillot, for the 1937 World Fair and now home to two museums.

The first is the **Musée d'Art Moderne de la Ville de Paris** (tel: 01 53 67 40 00; www.mam.paris.fr; Tue–Sun 10am–6pm; charge), the municipal collection of modern art, notable for

Matisse's *La Danse* (1932) and Raoul Dufy's *Fée de l'Electricité* (Electricity Fairy) mural.

In the opposite wing is the **Site de Création Contemporaraine** (tel: 01 47 23 54 01; www.palaisdetokyo.com; Tue–Sun noon–midnight; charge). Described as a 'laboratory for contemporary art', it focuses on young artists through exhibitions, performances and workshops. It also has a trendy restaurant, see ❶①.

MUSÉE DE LA MODE

On the other side of the road, in a mansion built by Gustave Eiffel, is the fashion museum, the **Musée de la Mode – Musée Galliera ❷** (10 avenue Pierre-1er-de-Serbie; tel: 01 56 52 86 00; daily Tue–Sun 10am–6pm when exhibitions are on only; charge). Drawing on its collection of 12,000 outfits and 60,000 accessories from the 18th century to the present, it shows two exhibitions each year, focusing on historic periods, themes and designers.

MUSÉE GUIMET

Continuing along avenue du Président Wilson, you come to place d'Iéna where, on your right at no. 6, is the **Musée National des Arts Asiatiques – Musée Guimet ❸**, the national

---

Food and Drink

① TOKYO EAT
Palais de Tokyo, avenue du Président Wilson, 8th; tel: 01 47 20 00 29; closed Mon; €€€
Design-conscious, fun and very popular, this restaurant has a contemporary menu that includes fusion and vegetarian dishes.

② BRASSERIE DE LA POSTE
54 rue de Longchamp, 16th; tel: 01 47 55 01 31; €€€
In a nice location, this pleasant, comfortable brasserie serves well-executed classic French dishes.

museum of Asian art (tel: 01 56 52 53 00; www. museeguimet.fr; daily except Tue 10am–6pm; charge). It was founded in 1889 as a museum of world religions by Émile Guimet, a 19th-century industrialist and traveller. With the addition of the Oriental collections from the Louvre, it now owns 45,000 items. Highlights include Chinese paintings from Dunhuang, the Treasure of Begram from Afghanistan and the Giant's Way, part of the temple complex from Angkor Wat, Cambodia. Many of these exhibits reflect France's colonial history and the work of French archaeologists.

For refreshments at this point, one option is to head for rue de Longchamp, to **Brasserie de la Poste**, see ⑪②.

PALAIS DE CHAILLOT

Back on avenue du Président Wilson, continuing west for a further 5 minutes brings you to place du Trocadéro and the **Palais de Chaillot ❹**. This huge Art Deco complex was designed by a trio of architects (Boileau, Carlu and Azema) and contains three museums, as well as a theatre. Note, however, that major renovations are ongoing, and sections may be inaccessible.

Cité de l'Architecture

First on your left, in the east wing, is the **Cité de l'Architecture et du Patrimoine** (tel: 01 58 51 52 00; www. citechaillot.fr; Mon, Wed, Fri–Sun 11am–7pm, Thur 11am–9pm; charge), housing the world's largest museum dedicated to architecture. The ground

floor charts France's architectural history through drawings, vintage photographs and life-size plaster casts of monuments, from cathedral portals and stained glass to Renaissance fountains. The second floor brings you into the present with thematic exhibitions.

Musée National de la Marine and Musée de l'Homme

In the west wing is the **Musée National de la Marine** (tel: 01 53 65 81 32, www. musee-marine.fr; Mon, Wed–Sun 10am–6pm, last admission at 5.15pm; charge). Displays of cannon barrels, cutlasses, early torpedoes, uniforms, models and paintings take you from ancient galleons to nuclear submarines.

Also in the west wing is the **Musée de l'Homme** (tel: 01 44 05 72 72; www. mnhn.fr), although this museum is closed for renovation until 2012.

Finish the route by walking down the steps behind the Palais de Chaillot to the gardens with their magnificent views of the Eiffel Tower *(see p.36)*.

Above from far left: at the Palais de Tokyo; Musée d'Art Moderne de la Ville de Paris.

Flood Marker
At Pont de l'Alma, look towards the Seine for the Zouave, a statue used as a river marker. If his toes get wet, Paris is put on flood alert. If his ankles go under water, roads adjacent to the river are closed, and if his hips are wet, an emergency floodplan is put into action.

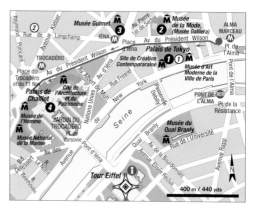

PÈRE LACHAISE

Wander in the maze of celebrity graves at Père Lachaise, then walk through Belleville, which, once a country village, then a workers' district, now offers an understated mix of cafés, artists' collectives, cottages and gardens.

DISTANCE 4km (2½ miles)
TIME Half a day
START Père Lachaise
END Place du Colonel Fabien
POINTS TO NOTE

The best metro station for the start of this tour is Philippe Auguste, by the cemetery's southwestern entrance.

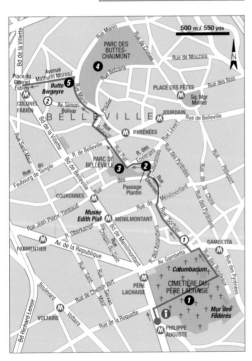

From metro Philippe Auguste, turn right on to boulevard de Ménilmontant, which is dominated by Paris's smartest address for the dead, the cemetery of **Père Lachaise ❶** (www.pere-lachaise. com; daily 9.30am–5.30pm; free). 'Residents' include Chopin, Molière and Rossini, as well as more recent luminaries: Edith Piaf, Gertrude Stein, Oscar Wilde, Jim Morrison and Yves Montand. At the main entrance on boulevard de Ménilmontant, visitors can pick up free maps pinpointing the more famous graves.

The cemetery is named after the confessor of Louis XIV, Père La Chaise (1624–1709), who lived in a Jesuit house on the site of the chapel. In 1804 it was established as a cemetery by Napoleon, although it was initially deemed too far from the city to attract many burials. As a marketing ploy, the administrators organised the transfer of the remains of writers La Fontaine and Molière, and, later, lovers Héloïse and Abélard. It seems to have worked, and today there are over 300,000 bodies buried here (and many more cremated remains).

CEMETERY TOUR

Walk up avenue Principale and turn right on to avenue du Puits to find the tomb of Abélard and Héloïse, with its

canopy composed of fragments of the abbey of Nogent-sur-Seine. In the 12th century, Héloïse was a student of the controversial theologian, Abélard, and secretly became his lover and wife. Her father's fury ended in Abélard being castrated and banished to a monastery, and Héloïse forced into a convent. However, they have left to posterity their letters, professing a pure and faithful love.

Artists and Writers

Retrace your steps to avenue Principale and make your way past the graves of Colette, Rossini and Alfred de Musset, up the shady paths to the chapel on the hilltop for a view over the chestnut trees. On the benches here you sometimes see old women feeding the cats who make their homes among the monuments.

Continue in the same direction, on avenue des Combattants Étrangers morts pour la France, passing the grave of the spiritualist Allan Kardec (where some leave odd mementoes or practise bizarre rites in front of his tomb) and on to the grand crematorium, bordered by the graves of Isadora Duncan, Maria Callas, Max Ophuls and Max Ernst. From here, if you have had enough, it is only a short walk further to an exit gate (toilets on the left-hand side), or, if you are ready for more, take a right turn along avenue Circulaire to the top (eastern) corner of the cemetery and the Mur des Fédérés.

Mur des Fédérés

This wall was where the last 147 anarchist rebels of the Paris Commune, a courageous uprising against Prussian

domination in 1871, were lined up and shot after their final resistance among the graves the night before. The bullet holes are still visible. Appropriately, also in this eastern corner is the Jardin du Souvenir, home to many monuments commemorating the dead of World War II, including victims of Auschwitz, Buchenwald and other concentration camps. There are also monuments to members of the French Resistance.

Lunch Stop

Leaving the cemetery behind via the exit nearest the crematorium, you emerge on to rue des Rondeaux. Turn left towards Gambetta metro station, left again on to place Martin Nadaud and then look for **rue Sorbier** on the far side. This leafy street takes you past some pleasant cafés and bistros including ⑪①.

BELLEVILLE

The tour now continues into **Belleville**. In the early 19th century, this was a fertile country village, whose springs were tapped to channel water into Paris; in the second half of the 19th century it evolved into a poor working-class area of the city and a forge of class agitation. In today's post-industrial

Above from far left: a family grave; no dogs allowed, even on a lead; statue; towards Victor Noir *(see below)*.

Victor Noir
Killed in a duel the day before he was to be married, this tragic hero is now venerated by women looking for love. According to popular belief, you only have to kiss the lips of the prostrate statue (avenue Transversale no. 2, 44th division) and slip a flower into the upturned hat and you will find a husband by the end of the year. The authorities are considering fencing it off due to excessive enthusiasm.

Above from left:
view over Paris from
the Parc de Belleville;
inside the trendy
Antoine et Lili
boutique, quai de
Valmy; canal views.

Poor Little Sparrow
According to legend,
Edith Piaf was born
under a lamp-post at
72 rue de Belleville.
The plaque over the
doorway reads,
'On the steps of
this house, on 19
December 1915, was
born, in the greatest
poverty, Piaf, whose
voice would later
take the world by
storm.' The tiny
Musée Edith Piaf at
5 rue Crespin-du-
Gast is a tribute to
the legendary queen
of French *chanson*.

landscape, the *quartier* is subject to gentrification, complete with the usual transient symptoms of art collectives and small-scale impromptu galleries.

Passage Plantin

Cross over rue de Ménilmontant on to rue Henri Chevreau, but not before looking left to take in the view towards the Centre Pompidou. Follow the road as it veers to the left and then turn right at rue des Couronnes, and then left down an alley, **Passage Plantin** ❷, with, behind railings, pretty houses that were typical of Belleville before the property developers moved in.

Parc de Belleville

At the other end of Passage Plantin, turn left on rue du Transvaal, which soon becomes rue Piat. Here, there is a fine view over the **Parc de Belleville** ❸ (8 or 9am–5.45pm in winter, 9.30pm in summer; free) and the wider city. The park cascades down the hillside, and is most attractive in its lowest reaches. Stop here if you want a rest.

Rue Rébeval

When you are ready to continue, resume rue Piat until you reach rue de Belleville. Just before you cross over on

---

Food and Drink 🍴
② **À LA BIERE**
104 avenue Simon-Bolivar,
19th; tel: 01 42 39 83 25; daily
noon–3pm, 7pm–1.30am; €
Friendly corner brasserie with an
impressively executed and extremely
well-priced *prix-fixe* menu.

---

to rue Rébeval, look for no. 72, outside which singer Edith Piaf was supposed to have been born under a lamp-post.

On rue Rébeval, watch out for the quirky brick building at nos 78–80, on the left-hand side. Although now the Paris-Belleville School of Architecture, this was once the Meccano factory and the source of many a child's constructive Christmas presents.

Butte Bergeyre

At this point, turn right on to rue Pradier, then left again on to avenue Simon-Bolivar (see 🍴②), which leads to the corner of the **Parc des Buttes-Chaumont** ❹. The park is covered in full in walk 12 *(see p.79)*, but you can end this tour here too, if you want.

Alternatively, follow the western edge of the park on rue Manin and turn left down avenue Mathurin Moreau. On the left-hand side is the **Butte Bergeyre** ❺, which before World War I was the site of a fairground full of merry-go-rounds and sideshows. It is now a quaint complex of lanes, houses and gardens clinging to the hillsides.

Place du Colonel Fabien

Rue Mathurin Moreau leads to place du Colonel Fabien, named after the *nom de guerre* of the French Communist resistance hero, Pierre Georges. Fittingly, the square is now dominated by the headquarters of the French Communist Party in a Modernist building designed by Brazilian architect Oscar Niemeyer and constructed from 1968 to 1971.

To return to central Paris, pick up the metro at Colonel-Fabien, nearby.

NORTHEAST PARIS

Catch a boat, cycle or stroll up the canal to an often-overlooked area of Paris that has lots to appeal to both children and adults: a science museum, 3-D cinema, submarine, music museum, beautiful parks and spectacular city views.

The route begins by following the Canal St-Martin from **place de la Bastille ❶** up to the northeast of Paris. Either start early and board a Canauxrama tour boat (tel: 01 42 39 15 00; www.canauxrama. com; reservations essential Oct–Mar; charge), or cycle or stroll up the canal towpaths (perhaps join the route near place de la République, where the canal crosses rue du Faubourg du Temple).

DISTANCE 9km (6½ miles)
TIME A full day
START Place de la Bastille
END Parc des Buttes-Chaumont
POINTS TO NOTE
If you choose to cycle up the canal, you can pick up free city-owned Vélib' bikes *(see p.102)* at place de la Bastille or place de la République.

CANAL CRUISE

If you choose the boat, the 2½-hour cruise begins at the **Arsenal Marina ❷** (once a busy commercial port), by 50 boulevard de la Bastille. Departures are at 9.45am and 2.30pm daily, and commentaries are in both English and French. Sit on the top deck for the best views, though take a jumper in case it gets chilly en route. (Note that cruises also run in the opposite direction, from the Bassin de la Villette to the Bastille.)

Going Underground

Napoleon commissioned the canal partly to allow more water into the city centre and earn the citizens' affection; in those days average daily consumption was one litre (¼ gallon) per person, as opposed to 200 litres (53 gallons) today.

At place de la Bastille, the canal goes underground, emerging again beyond **place de la République ❸**. As you glide under the city, you pass through a strip of the canal that is lit by pave-

Point Ephémère
On the Canal St-Martin is one of the city's foremost alternative cultural venues, the Point Ephémère (200 quai de Valmy, tel: 01 40 34 02 48; www.point ephemere.org). A 1930s former warehouse, it has been converted into artists' studios, a club, music studios, a gallery and a café. Another nice café on quai de Valmy is Chez Prune, see ⑪①.

Food and Drink 🍴
① CHEZ PRUNE
71 quai de Valmy, 10th; tel: 01 42 41 30 47; Mon–Sat 8am–2am, Sun 10am–2am; €
Watch the world go by at this cornerstone of trendy Canal St-Martin. Respectable food at lunch time and tapas-style snacks at night.

Left: Canal St-Martin.

Above from left:
on the banks of the
Canal St-Martin; la Vil-
lette's old market hall.

ment gratings that send shafts of light
down to the water. The different colours
of mortar indicate where restoration
work has been carried out; the area
overhead has been untouched since the
canal was built.

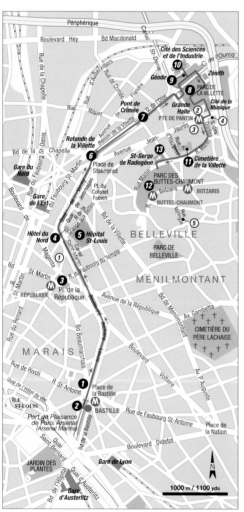

Hôtel du Nord

At **quai de Valmy** and **quai de Jem-mapes**, you emerge amid trees and
gardens into a unique Parisian land-scape, punctuated with 19th-century
iron footbridges and locks. On the
right bank is the **Hôtel du Nord ❹**,
the inspiration for Marcel Carné's
1938 film of the same name, and now
an atmospheric bar and bistro. In the
evenings, it is a venue for Anglophone
stand-up comedy.

Behind it is the **Hôpital St-Louis
❺**, built from 1607 to shelter plague
victims, who were previously housed in
tents and quarantined from the rest of
the city. Adjacent, on rue de la
Grange-aux-Belles, are two note-worthy *chanson* cafés for evening wine
and song, Chez Adel (no. 10) and
Apostrophe (no. 23).

Rotonde de la Villette

Going north, at place de Stalingrad you
reach the **Rotonde de la Villette ❻**,
one of Claude Nicholas Ledoux's
beautifully designed tollhouses (now
hosting exhibitions). It marks the start
of the **Bassin de la Villette**, built for
Napoleon in 1808, and bordered by
stylish new cinemas, beautiful old ware-houses and some less appealing 1960s
and '70s high-rise blocks. In true post-industrial fashion, some warehouses
here have been reclaimed by artists'
cooperatives as studio space.

At the top end of the basin is an
ingenious piece of 19th-century engi-neering: a hydraulic lifting bridge, the
Pont de Crimée ❼, which displaces a
whole section of road. Just beyond the

port is the Parc de la Villette, where the canal divides into the canals de l'Ourcq and St-Denis, and where the boat ride comes to an end.

PARC DE LA VILLETTE

The **Parc de la Villette** ❽ (avenues Corentin-Cariou and Jean-Jaurès; tel: 01 40 03 75 75; www.villette.com; daily 9.30am–6.30pm; free) was created in 1986 as one of François Mitterrand's *grands projets (see p.30)*, on a 50-ha (136-acre) site, where the city's meat market once stood.

Géode

On the left of the canal is the **Géode** ❾, a polished-steel sphere, which looks rather like something from outer space. Inside, the hemispheric theatre has one of the world's largest screens and dizzily slanted seating. Movies are made specially for this huge screen, many on a natural science theme.

Cité des Sciences

The **Cité des Sciences et de l'Industrie** ❿ (tel: 01 40 05 70 00; www.cite-sciences.fr; Tue–Sat 10am–6pm, Sun 10am–7pm; charge except for ground-floor exhibits in main hall), or science museum, was created by the architect Adrien Fainsilber from the shell of an unfinished slaughterhouse building.

Inside, there is plenty to see, particularly for children (of all ages): try out the jet-pack simulator for armchair astronauts, experience the sensations of space sickness or weightlessness, practise on a flight simulator, and perform experiments using mirrors, electricity and tricks of perspective. There are other exhibits on the origins of life, the underwater world, plant life, and there are even robotic animals in a cybernetic zoo.

The **Planetarium** runs several programmes a day. There is an extra charge for these: buy your tickets as soon as you arrive, since they sell out quickly.

The Park

The park itself is the largest in Paris, spread over more than 35ha (86 acres). It was designed by Swiss landscape architect Bernard Tschumi as 11 gardens, each with a different theme. Children should enjoy the Dragon's Garden, the Garden of the Winds and the Garden of Childhood Fears, with its fairy-tale mystery, dark colours and engaging sound system. Adults may prefer the subtlety of the Garden of Shadows and the beauty of the Garden of Bamboos.

In summer, the Triangle Meadow is a nice place to sit and enjoy a picnic. You can even watch an outdoor movie here, on a giant inflatable screen – around 60,000 spectators came to the 2008 screenings.

At regular intervals in the park, you will spot bright-red enamelled-steel buildings, which are contemporary versions of 18th-century French architectural fantasies or follies. Each one looks different and is devoted to a special activity; the Folie Argonaute, for example, leads you to a real submarine that arrived via the Canal de l'Ourcq.

Cité des Enfants
The Parc de la Villette's Cité des Enfants has lots of fun, interactive attractions for children, with areas divided according to age (2–7 and 5–12 year olds).

Above from left:
Parc de la Villette; a
concert at the Zénith;
Guignols, Parc des
Buttes-Chaumont.

**Musée de
la Musique**
Highlights of this
excellent collection
include violins by
Stradivarius,
trumpets by Johann
Wilhelm Has, and
instruments owned
by the composers
Fauré, Berlioz and
Chopin. There is
even a full Javanese
Gamelan orchestra.

Zénith

Next to the northern bridge is a large,
grey, solid-looking tent, the **Zénith**, a
concert hall that can seat up to 6,300
people and is best known as the centre
of Paris's thriving rap scene. Opposite, a new-wave circus performs below
the big top of **Espace Chapiteaux**.

On the east side of the canal is **La
Grande Halle**, a fine example of 19th-
century iron architecture. Until 1974 it
housed France's national meat market,
but it was rendered obsolete by modern
refrigeration and poor design – the
cows could not get up the steps – and
is now an exhibition space. Shows
range from the prestigious, often controversial Paris Biennale contemporary

art show to the International Architectural Fair, to fashion shows. Nearby is
the **Maison de la Villette**, home to an
exhibition on the history of the park.

Cité de la Musique

On the extreme southeastern edge of
the park is the **Cité de la Musique**.
Designed by architect Christian de
Portzamparc, the complex includes the
Musée de la Musique (tel: 01 44 84
45 00, www.citedelamusique.fr; Tue–
Sat noon–6pm, Sun 10am–6pm;
charge) and a stylish café, see 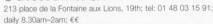②.

The museum charts the development
of classical, jazz and folk music and
houses an impressive collection of more
than 4,500 musical instruments. On
the other side of the Grande Halle is
Portzamparc's Conservatoire, a music
and dance conservatory, where you can
attend concerts by top performers.

CIMETIÈRE DE LA VILLETTE

Leaving La Cité de la Musique and Parc
de la Villette, cross avenue Jean-Jaurès
(perhaps stopping for lunch at the epi-
cure's valhalla, **Au Boeuf Couronné**, see
🍴③, or a lighter meal at **Le Local
Rock**, 🍴④). Note that there is a pick-
up/drop-off point (Station Vélib') for
city bikes on Jean-Jaurès at this point.

Head down Sente des Dorées and
then take the second right on to rue
Manin for the pleasant 15-minute
walk to the Parc des Buttes-Chaumont.
On the way, a minor detour on to rue
d'Hautpoul on your right brings you
to the **Cimetière de la Villette** ⓫
(mid-Mar–Oct 8am–6pm, Nov–mid-

Food and Drink 🍴

② CAFÉ DE LA MUSIQUE
213 place de la Fontaine aux Lions, 19th; tel: 01 48 03 15 91;
daily 8.30am–2am; €€
Pleasant restaurant with an attractive summer terrace at the
entrance of the Parc de la Villette. Mix of nouvelle cuisine and
classic brasserie fare.

③ AU BOEUF COURONNÉ
188 avenue Jean-Jaurès, 19th; tel: 01 42 39 44 44; closed
Sun; €€
Outstanding restaurant just across the road from where
the meat market (now the music Conservatoire) used to be.
Specialises in butchery: every kind of steak, bone marrow with
toast and *tête de veau* (veal's head). Not for the faint-hearted.

④ LE LOCAL ROCK
206 avenue Jean-Jaurès, 19th; tel: 01 42 08 06 65; closed
Sun; €
Simple, great-value bistro decorated with kitsch pop memorabilia.

⑤ RESTAURANT L'HERMÈS
23 rue Mélingue, 19th; tel: 01 42 39 94 70; closed Sun, Mon; €€
Superb-value restaurant just south of the Parc des Buttes-
Chaumont. Good food with a southwestern flavour.

SEANCES :
(Par beau temps)
MERCREDI
à 15 H 30

SAMEDI
DIMANCHE
ET FETES
à 16 Heures

Mar 8am–5.30pm; free). Through a monumental gateway you find a mini version of Père Lachaise cemetery with monumental 19th-century tombs set under a canopy of trees.

PARC DES BUTTES-CHAUMONT

The **Parc des Buttes-Chaumont** ⓬ (daily: Oct–Apr 7am–8pm, May–Aug 7am–10pm, Sept 7am–9pm; free), one of the finest parks in Paris, was built by Baron Haussmann in the 1860s on the site of a rubbish dump and gypsum quarry. The uneven ground provided a perfect setting for a wooded, rocky terrain, and a lake has been created around an artificial 50m (165ft) 'mountain', which is capped by a Roman-style temple, with a waterfall and a cave containing fake stalactites. Ice-skating, boating and donkey rides are also on offer, and the puppet show or 'Guignols' in the open-air theatre has been a popular attraction for more than 150 years (weather permitting, shows are on Wed, Sat and Sun at 4pm and 5pm).

Russian Church

On the western side of the park, near where you entered, is the atmospheric Russian church of **St-Serge de Radogène** ⓭ (www.saint-serge.net; irregular opening hours; free). You approach it through a gateway at 93 rue de Crimée. Originally built as a Protestant church in 1861, it was acquired by the Russian Orthodox Church in 1924 to minister to the influx of Russian immigrants

fleeing the Revolution. The elaborate wooden porch was built at this stage. Inside, there are icons and candelabra, and wonderful wall-paintings of scenes of Noah's ark, the burning bush and other stories.

BACK TO CENTRAL PARIS

To get back into town from here, you can take the metro from Buttes-Chaumont or Botzaris. Alternatively, take bus no. 75, which goes to the Centre Pompidou and Hôtel de Ville. The bus begins back at place de la Porte de Pantin, near where you left the Parc de la Villette, but has various stops at points around Parc des Buttes-Chaumont. In common with most Parisian buses, it only runs until about 8.30pm.

If you would like to have dinner before leaving the area, consider **Restaurant Hermès**, ⑪⑤.

Above: St-Serge.

Below: the Géode at the Parc de la Villette.

BERCY AND VINCENNES

Follow a pretty garden path along a former railway viaduct towards the regeneration quarter of Bercy. Choose between exploring the Bois de Vincennes or the old centre of the wine trade with its bars, cafés, cinemas and park.

DISTANCE 7.25km (4½ miles)
TIME Half a day
START Opéra Bastille
END Parc de Vincennes or Bercy
POINTS TO NOTE
From the Parc de Vincennes, the best metro station is Porte Dorée. From Cour St-Emilion, you can catch the 'Meteor' metro line (no. 14); the first line to be built since 1935, it has fully automated, driver-less trains.

Cinema in Bercy

The ill-fated, long-empty American Center, designed by architect Frank Gehry, has happily now become the home of the Cinémathèque Française (51 rue de Bercy; tel: 01 71 19 33 33; www.cinema thequefrancaise. com; daily except Tue, see website for times): a film museum, repertory cinema and film archive. At the eastern edge of the park at Bercy Village is another cinema, the 18-screen Ciné Cité.

Starting at the **Opéra National de la Bastille ❶**, walk down rue de Lyon and take avenue Daumesnil on your left. You will soon reach some steps, signposted Promenade Plantée. At the top begins a walk along a former railway viaduct, built in 1859, and now transformed into a garden with a succession of wrought-iron arches, and roses, trees and shrubs where steam trains once chugged.

Underneath the arches, dubbed the **Viaduc des Arts ❷** (15–121 avenue Daumesnil), are the shops of jewellery designers, cabinet makers, and even a French hunting-horn maker, continuing the traditions of this artisan-quarter of town. At the end of the promenade is the **Jardin de Reuilly ❸** with its ponds, waterfall and wooden bridge. Just before the garden is **Comme Cochons**, see ⑪①, on rue de Charenton.

At this point, you have a choice: either continue along avenue Daumesnil to a remarkable aquarium and the vast Bois de Vincennes, with its lakes, château and zoo, or head south to the Parc de Bercy and Bercy Village, where wine warehouses have been converted into a bustling centre for restaurants and bars.

BOIS DE VINCENNES

If heading for the Bois de Vincennes, continue along avenue Daumesnil, past the bizarre Église du St-Ésprit at no. 186 (a 1920s concrete copy of Hagia Sophia in Istanbul), until you come to the **Palais de la Porte Dorée ❹** (tel: 01 53 59 58 60; Tue–Fri 10am–5.15pm, Sat–Sun 10am–7pm; charge) on the left-hand side at no. 293, with

its extraordinary basement aquarium (www.aquarium-portedoree.fr). It also houses the **Cité Nationale de l'Histoire de l'Immigration** (www.histoire-immigration.fr), a cultural institute on the role of immigrants in France over the last 200 years.

Bois de Vincennes and Parc Floral

Continue on avenue Daumesnil to the **Bois de Vincennes ❺** (tel: 01 43 28 41 59; www.boisdevincennes.com; daily dawn–dusk; free), Paris's largest green space. Attractions include boating, cycle paths, a Buddhist temple, zoo (closed for renovation until 2012), racetrack, baseball pitch and the Cartoucherie Theatre. The **Parc Floral** (a park within the wood; charge) has free jazz and classical concerts on summer weekends, a picnic area, playground and crazy golf.

Château de Vincennes

On the northern edge of the park is the **Château de Vincennes** (tel: 01 48 08 31 20; www.chateau-vincennes.fr; Sept–Apr: daily 10am–5pm, May–Aug until 6pm; charge), completed by Charles V in 1370. Over the centuries its use has changed from palace to prison to porcelain factory to arsenal. The château was heavily damaged during World War II. Now restored, it houses a museum.

BERCY

For the alternative option of **Bercy Village**, bear right after the Jardin de Reuilly on to rue de Charenton, and turn right on to rue Prudhon. Follow the road over the railway, past the church and continue to the **Parc de Bercy ❻** (summer: Mon–Fri 8am–9pm, Sat–Sun 9am–9pm; winter: Mon–Fri 8am–5.30pm, Sat–Sun 9am–5.30pm; free).

At the western end of the park is the rather ugly new Ministère de l'Economie et du Budget and the Palais Omnisports, a 17,000-seat stadium used for events from basketball to opera to rock festivals. Also within the park is the **Cinémathèque Française ❼** *(see left)*.

Bercy Village

As late as the 1980s wine was unloaded from barges at Bercy. Forty-two *chais* (wine warehouses) have been cleaned up and reopened as restaurants, wine bars and shops, and some have been converted into the **Pavillons de Bercy ❽**, containing the **Musée des Arts Forains ❾** (by appointment only; tel: 01 43 40 16 22), home to a collection of fairground music and Venetian carnival salons. Of the restaurants nearby, try **Chai 33**, see ①②.

Above from far left: outside Chai 33, Bercy; blooms in the Parc Floral; Cinémathèque Française; Stade de Bercy.

'New' Left Bank
Opposite Bercy on the so-called 'New' Left Bank is the Bibliothèque Nationale de France – François Mitterrand. Opened in 1997, it cost over $1billion and is more expensive to maintain than the Louvre. Its four 90m (295ft) -high glass towers are intended to evoke open books. The regenerated area is now home to many attractive bars and cafés, including several riverside ones.

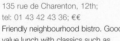

WESTERN PARIS

This is a posh part of town and off the main tourist track. Its attractions include pretty parks, Art Nouveau and Modernist architecture, Balzac's house and museums of wine and Impressionist art.

DISTANCE 3.5km (2¼ miles)
TIME A full day
START Passy metro station
END Musée Marmottan or the Bois de Boulogne (*see below*)
POINTS TO NOTE
If you end the tour after the Musée Marmottan, pick up the metro at La Muette; if you continue to the Bois de Boulogne, the metro is at Porte Dauphine (to the north) and Porte d'Auteuil (to the south).

The 16th *arrondissement* constitutes a sizeable slice of western Paris and is full of smart residences occupied by wealthy inhabitants. Just adjacent (though outside the Périphérique) is the Bois de Boulogne, an 860-ha (2,125-acre) expanse of woods and gardens laid out under town planner Baron Haussmann. This is one of the reasons that the 16th has long been popular with Parisians; avenue Foch, perhaps the most expensive residential street in the capital, leads straight to its gates.

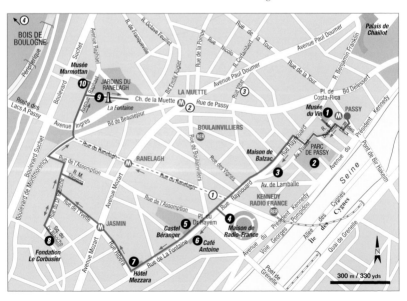

MUSÉE DU VIN

Catch the metro to Passy, and, as you leave the station, turn right down the steps. Turn right again at the bottom, then right a third time at rue des Eaux. This street is named after the mineral springs where people came to take cures for anaemia in the days when Passy was a country village. Ironically, at the end of this street, at no. 5 square Charles Dickens, is the **Musée du Vin ❶** (tel: 01 45 25 63 26; www.museeduvinparis. com; Tue–Sun 10am–6pm; charge).

Here, within the cellars of a wine-producing monastery destroyed in the Revolution, you are guided through the wine-making process. There are also regular wine tastings (some in English) and a restaurant (lunch only), with wines selected for each course.

As you leave the museum, turn right on to rue Charles Dickens and then walk straight on to the modest **Parc de Passy ❷**. After recovering from the effects of any wine you may have drunk at the museum, climb the steps on the north side of the park up to rue Ray-nouard and turn left.

MAISON DE BALZAC

On your left, at no. 47, is the **Maison de Balzac ❸** (tel: 01 42 24 56 38; www.paris.fr/musees; Tue–Sun 10am–6pm; permanent collection free). The writer Honoré de Balzac (1799–1850), a self-styled 'quill and ink galley slave', lived here in secret for seven years, from 1840 (under the assumed name of Monsieur Breugnol, one of the characters in his

novels) in order to escape his creditors. On the simple table in his study he worked day and night on *La Comédie Humaine*, his vast series of 91 novels and stories peopled with thousands of interconnected characters.

Another room is devoted to Madame Hanska, the wealthy Russian widow who teased Balzac for 18 years with the prospect of marriage and instant credit relief. She became his wife just five months before his death.

RADIO FRANCE

Now continue in the same direction on rue Raynouard to the **Maison de Radio-France ❹** (entrance on far side, at 116 avenue du Président Kennedy; tel: 01 56 40 15 16; www.radiofrance.fr; tours daily except Sun by reservation only; charge), the Orwellian home of the state radio station and broad-casting bureaucracy opened in 1963.

ALTERNATIVE ROUTES

At this point you have a choice of routes. If you want to fast forward to the Musée Marmottan *(see p.85)*, turn right and walk up rue du Ranelagh, past **L'Antenne**, see 🍴①. At the end of the road, go through the passage and

Above from far left: entrance to the Maison de Balzac; street sign reflecting the area's past as the site of a spring; bust of the novelist in his former garden; at the front gate.

Writer's Brew
To keep himself awake, Balzac drank around 40 cups of coffee a day, and his well-used cafetière is displayed in one of the rooms at the Maison de Balzac. Outside, there is an attractive garden, with seating, lots of sheltered corners and excellent views over the city.

turn right over the zebra crossing to the Jardins du Ranelagh. The museum is on the left, just off avenue Raphael.

If, on the other hand, you are interested in taking a detour for an hour or so in order to see some fine examples of Art Nouveau and Modernist architecture, go up rue La Fontaine.

ARCHITECTURE TOUR

Art Nouveau
Rue Jean de La Fontaine is home to the city's best examples of Art Nouveau architecture by Hector Guimard, the man who was responsible for the flamboyant entrances to metro stations such as the one at Abbesses *(see p.65)*. On your right at no. 14 is the extraordinary **Castel Béranger ❺** *(see left)*. Guimard also designed the more modest buildings at nos 19 and 21, and

the tiny **Café Antoine ❻** at no. 17 on your left. Further up, at no. 60, is **Hôtel Mezzara ❼**, whose wonderful interior steals the limelight from the free art exhibitions it hosts.

Soon after, turn right on to rue Ribera, which then becomes rue de l'Yvette.

Modernism
At the top of rue de l'Yvette is rue du Dr Blanche, with two examples of Modernist architecture. Turn left for square du Dr Blanche and the **Fondation Le Corbusier ❽** *(see below)* on your left. Next, turn right, and on your right is rue Mallet-Stevens, almost entirely made up of houses by Robert Mallet-Stevens (1886–1945). No. 10, with its stained-glass stairwell, is very fine.

Now continue north up rue du Dr Blanche and turn left at rue de l'Assomption, and then right on boulevard

Castel Béranger
This Art Nouveau creation was Hector Guimard's first building commission, and he designed everything: the mosaic floors, the wallpaper, even the stoves. Note the green seahorses climbing the facade, and the faces on the balconies, which are supposed to be a self-portrait, inspired by Japanese figures, to ward off evil spirits. Despite its lavish decoration, Castel Béranger was built as a cheap lodging house.

Le Corbusier

Although Charles-Edouard Jeanneret (1887–1965), known as Le Corbusier, developed his brand of Modernism in the interests of providing better living conditions for inhabitants of crowded cities, he has been heavily criticised for inspiring the building of soulless tower blocks surrounded by featureless wastelands. However, the two adjoining houses that make up the Fondation Le Corbusier (8–10 square du Dr Blanche; tel: 01 42 88 41 53; www.fondationlecorbusier.asso.fr; Mon 1.30–6pm, Tue–Thur 10am–6pm, Fri–Sat 10am–5pm; charge) show how elegant and light his buildings can be. Inside are exhibition spaces for his drawings, plans, furniture and paintings. It is also possible to visit the apartment occupied by Le Corbusier from 1934 to 1965 in the nearby Immeuble Molitor (24 rue Nungesser et Coli, 16th; tel: 01 46 03 32 90; by appointment only Sat 10am–1pm, 1.30–5pm).

de Montmorency. Soon on your left is an inconspicuous path taking you through to avenue Ingres. Turn right and over the zebra crossing you will find the **Jardins du Ranelagh** ❾, an appealing park for young children, as it retains several old-fashioned carousels, including a lovely wind-up one.

MUSÉE MARMOTTAN

West of the gardens on the corner of rue Louis-Boilly (at no. 2) is the **Musée Marmottan** ❿ (tel: 01 44 96 50 33 www.marmottan.com; Tue–Sun 10am–6pm, Thur till 9pm; charge), which gives an unrivalled overview of the career of Claude Monet (1840–1926). In the gallery downstairs, you start with *Impression, Soleil Levant (Impression, Sunrise),* which gave the Impressionist Movement its name. Monet's ideas then evolve up to his last, almost abstract, *Nymphéas (Waterlily)* paintings.

Thanks to other donations, Monet's contemporaries are also well represented. On the first floor are works by Pissarro, Renoir, Manet, Morisot, Caillebotte and Gauguin. On the ground floor, slightly incongruously, there is a fine collection of First Empire furniture as well as a section on medieval illuminated manuscripts.

PARKS AND GARDENS

With the route nearing its end, you have a choice of walking back through the Ranelagh gardens to cafés, restaurants and the metro home, or strolling through the vast **Bois de Boulogne**

(24 hours; free) to the west beyond the Marmottan.

For the first option, walk back towards town along chaussée de la Muette. On the way you pass the **statue of La Fontaine** with the fox and crow from one of his fables, and, as you leave the park, the lively **La Gare**, see 🍴②, on your right. A little further west, along rue de Passy, then left on to rue Vital, is **Chez Géraud**, see 🍴③.

Bois de Boulogne

For the second option, if it is a pleasant summer evening, consider a meal at **Le Chalet des Îles**, see 🍴④. Otherwise, seek out **Les Serres d'Auteuil**, to the south (near the Roland Garros tennis centre). These romantic glasshouses, opened in 1895, offer seasonal displays of orchids and begonias as well as a tropical pavilion with palm trees, birds and a pool of Japanese carp.

Above from far left:
Modernist signs;
house by Mallet-Stevens on the road
of the same name;
doorknocker at the
Musée Marmottan;
Monet's *Impression,
Soleil Levant.*

En Vélo
One of the best ways to explore the Bois de Boulogne is by bicycle. Borrow one for free through the Velib' scheme *(see p.102)*; there are pick-up/drop-off points by the main park gates.

Food and Drink 🍴

② LA GARE
19 chaussée de la Muette, 16th; tel: 01 42 15 15 31; daily; €€
Former railway station, where the ticket office has become the bar, and the platforms dining areas. The quality and price of the food are surprisingly reasonable for the chichi 16th.

③ CHEZ GÉRAUD
31 rue Vital, 16th; tel: 01 45 20 33 00; Mon–Fri; €€–€€€
Classic bistro serving hearty regional cuisine, with the emphasis on roasted meat and game dishes. Excellent service.

④ LE CHALET DES ÎLES
Lac Inférieur, Bois de Boulogne, 16th; tel: 01 42 88 04 69; www.lechaletdesiles.net; Tue–Sun (Sun lunch only) and Mon in summer; €€€€
A short boat ride to the island on the more northerly of the park's two lakes leads to this pretty chalet, transplanted from Switzerland by Napoleon III for his wife. Gorgeous setting.

LA DÉFENSE

Named after a stand against the Prussians in 1870, La Défense is now a business district dominated by the Grande Arche, which completes the Royal Axis that links the Louvre, Tuileries, Champs-Élysées and Arc de Triomphe.

DISTANCE 1.5km (1 mile)

TIME 3 hours

START Les Quatre Temps Shopping Centre, La Défense

END Espace Raymond Moretti

POINTS TO NOTE

Take either RER line A or metro line 1 to La Défense-Grande Arche, where the station exits lead you into Les Quatre Temps commercial centre. Doors to the Grande Arche are signed.

What's in a Name?

La Défense takes its name from the bronze sculpture by Louis-Ernest Barrias (1841–1905) that was erected here in 1883 to commemorate the defence of Paris against the Prussian army in 1870.

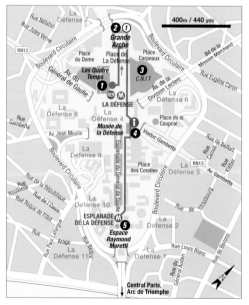

La Défense was designated a business district as early as 1958, but it was not until the 1980s that its reputation was secured. Nowadays, more than 150,000 people work in the district, and about three-quarters of the top 20 French companies have their headquarters here, as do around a dozen of the top 50 companies in the world. And even though La Défense was officially completed in 1988 after 20 years' work, many of the original buildings are now being replaced with more advanced constructions as part of a grand plan entitled 'La Défense 2006–2015'. Recent developments have included a 40-storey tower by Pei Cobb Freed and a church by Franck Hammoutène.

GRANDE ARCHE

The metro exit brings you into **Les Quatre Temps** ❶ shopping centre, an outlet for clothes, electronics and food. Head for daylight, following signs to the **Grande Arche** ❷ (tel: 01 49 07 27 55; www.grandearche.com; daily 10am–7pm, last lift at 6.30pm; charge). More than any other building, it is this great behemoth, designed by Danish architect Johan Otto von Spreckelsen, that put La Défense on the map, and in so doing became a symbol of François Mitterrand's 'progressive vision for the 1980s'.

Royal Axis and Impressive Statistics
From the steps of the arch, you can take in the Royal Axis *(see p.30)* that runs straight to the Arc de Triomphe, heads along the Champs-Élysées and Tuileries, and ends at the Arc de Triomphe du Carrousel and the Louvre.

Intriguingly, the arch is positioned 6.33 degrees off the line of the axis. It has been suggested that this relates to the Louvre Pyramid (similarly off-line), or that it emphasises the depth of the structure, since from head-on it can seem two-dimensional. In fact, it seems that it was simply due to problems in siting the foundations.

The size of the arch is symbolic, measuring 100m by 100m (330 sq ft), the same dimensions as the Cour Carrée at the Louvre.

Lift to the Top
It is worth taking a lift to the top: two glass bubbles whisk visitors up to the roof at vertiginous speeds, through the symbolic 'cloud', a canvas net suspended between the twin towers and designed to cut down wind resistance. On the roof terrace, artist Jean-Pierre Raynaud's *Carte du Ciel* (Map of the Sky) resembles an enormous sundial. On the 35th floor is an option for a late breakfast or lunch, see ⑴①. Also at the top is a museum charting the development of the computer, with 200 items on display.

SCULPTURE PARK

Wander down from the Grande Arche to explore the area a little further. On your left as you head southeast is the CNIT ❸ (Centre National des Industries et des Techniques; 2 place de la Défense), a huge conference and exhibition centre, identifiable by its vast vaulted roof.

Next head for the tourist information centre, the *espace info*, on the esplanade du Général de Gaulle, ahead of you. In the basement is the **Musée de la Défense** ❹ (15 place de la Défense; tel: 01 47 74 84 24; daily 10am–6pm, Sat till 7pm; free), exploring 50 years of architectural innovation in this district. The museum also gives information on the outdoor sculpture park at la Défense. There are over 70 signed pieces on display including works by Miró, César and Calder.

More art is on offer at 2 esplanade du Général du Gaulle, at the **Espace Raymond Moretti** ❺ (Mon–Fri noon–5pm). Named after the French painter (1931–2005), the gallery is dedicated to changing exhibitions of contemporary art and photography.

Continue down the esplanade du Général du Gaulle to reach the metro back into central Paris.

Above from far left: Les Quatre Temps; the Grande Arche; ornamental lake; symbolic 'cloud' beneath the arch.

Spiderman
In 1999, Alain 'Spiderman' Robert climbed the arch's exterior, using only his bare hands and feet, and with no safety equipment of any kind – a method that cannot be condoned. On the subject of bugs, the arch also featured in the 2004 film *Godzilla: Final Wars*, in which it was destroyed by a giant insect, Kamacuras.

Food and Drink 🍴

① RESTAURANT Ô110
35th floor, Grande Arche; tel: 01 49 07 27 32; restaurant: Mon–Fri 11.30am–4.30pm, brasserie: 10am–6pm; €€
Typical of most restaurants in this area, Ô110 caters mainly to a business crowd with its slick, modern menu. However, the location, 110m (360ft) up, within the Grande Arche itself, is reason enough to single it out. The lift up the arch is also free to restaurant customers.

MALMAISON

In the quiet suburb of Rueil-Malmaison is one of the most appealing châteaux within easy reach of the French capital: Malmaison, the stylish and evocative former home of Josephine Bonaparte, first wife of Napoleon I.

Bois-Préau

Tickets to Malmaison also cover entry to Bois-Préau (Musée du Château de Bois Préau, 1 avenue de l'Impératrice Joséphine, Rueil-Malmaison; tel: 01 41 29 05 55), although, at the time of writing, this château, now a Napoleonic museum, was temporarily closed for renovation.

DISTANCE 24km (15 miles) rtn

TIME A full day

START Château de Malmaison

END Rueil-Malmaison

POINTS TO NOTE

The distance above is for the journey from central Paris. To reach the start point by public transport take RER line A to La Défense-Grande Arche, then bus 258 to the 'Le Château' stop; by car, take Route National 13 from Paris. There is parking at the château.

To reach the **Château de Malmaison** ❶ (rue du Château; tel: 01 41 29 05 55; www.chateau-malmaison.fr; Wed–Mon Apr–Sept 10am–12.30pm, 1.30–5.45pm, Sat–Sun till 6.15pm, Oct–Mar 10am–12.30pm, 1.30–5.15pm, Sat–Sun till 5.45pm; charge), follow the instructions in the grey box on the left. The journey takes around 40 minutes.

BACKGROUND

The palace passed through various hands until, in 1799, it caught the eye of Madame Bonaparte. She reputedly had to borrow money for the down-payment from the previous owner's steward – a sum that Napoleon (furious at his wife's spending) repaid on his return from conquering Egypt.

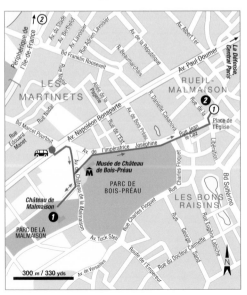

Food and Drink 🍴

① LE BEAUHARNAIS

29 place de l'Eglise, Rueil-Malmaison; tel: 01 47 51 02 88; €

Nice brasserie in the church square with outdoor seating in summer.

② RESTAURANT DE LA MAISON FOURNAISE

Ile des Impressionistes, 3 rue du Bac, Chatou; tel: 01 30 71 41 91; €€

This island makes a glorious spot for lunch or dinner, particularly in summer, on the lovely waterside terrace.

Josephine engaged the services of up-and-coming architectural duo, Percier and Fontaine, to renovate the building in the fashionable neoclassical style (with simple, geometric forms and minimal extraneous decoration), and in 1805 she employed L.M. Berthault to work on the surrounding park.

Country Retreat and Office

While Malmaison was initially used by the consular couple as a country retreat, by 1800 Napoleon was spending an increasing amount of time here. But in 1809, since Josephine could not provide an heir (despite having two children by her first marriage), Napoleon nullified the marriage and gave his former wife the Malmaison estate, plus a pension of 5 million francs a year. It was here that she spent most of her time until her death in 1814.

TOUR OF THE CHÂTEAU

Highlights on the **ground floor** include a monumental billiard table, two paintings by Gérard and Girodet on the subject of Ossian in the drawing room, and Josephine's harp topped by an Imperial eagle in the music room. Note also the delicate Pompeïian-style paintings on the stuccoed dining-room walls, Napoleon's striped, tent-style council room and the library with its ceiling dotted with classical-style busts of authors from Ovid to Voltaire.

First and Second Floors

The **first floor** houses the private apartments, although little of what is now on display is original: much has been acquired from the Palais des Tuileries and other former royal residences. Most striking on this floor are the paintings of Napoleon and Josephine by artists including Gérard, Riesener, Bacler d'Albe and David. The **second floor** is dedicated to displaying the contents of the former Empress's wardrobe, for which she was renowned.

THE GARDEN

Next, walk round to the back of the building to admire the park, beautifully landscaped in the English country-garden style. Josephine grew 200 plants never before cultivated in France. Still here is the massive cedar tree on the right as you stand with your back to the house; it was planted in 1800 to celebrate Napoleon's victory at Marengo.

OTHER ATTRACTIONS

Also worth a pit stop are the **Pavillon Osiris** (Osiris Pavilion), with its decorative-arts collection, and the **Pavillon des Voitures** (Carriage Pavilion), showcasing Napoleon's field landau used in his Russian campaign and the hearse used on St-Helena for his funeral.

Although there are no restaurants at the château itself, it is a 15-minute walk into little **Rueil-Malmaison ❷**, where **Le Beauharnais,** see ⑪①, is an inviting option. If time allows, take the 20-minute drive (or a taxi) north to Chatou and the small island in the middle of the Seine that is home to the **Restaurant de la Maison Fournaise**, see ⑪②.

VERSAILLES

Described by the writer and philosopher Voltaire as 'a masterpiece of bad taste and magnificence', Versailles, symbol of pre-Revolutionary decadence, offers a vivid encounter with French history.

Opening Times

Château: Apr–Oct
Tue–Sun 9am–
6.30pm, Nov–Mar
Tue–Sun 9am–
5.30pm. Petit Trianon,
Hameau and Grand
Trianon: Apr–Oct
daily noon–6.30pm,
Nov–Mar daily noon–
5.30pm. Last entry
30 mins prior to
closing. Gardens:
Apr–Oct daily 8am–
8.30pm, Nov–Mar
Tue–Sun 8am–6pm.
Grandes Eaux
Musicales shows:
Apr–Sept Sat–Sun;
charge except
gardens in winter.

DISTANCE 42km (26 miles) rtn

TIME A full day

START/END Versailles

POINTS TO NOTE

To reach the palace by public transport take the RER line C to Versailles-Rive-Gauche-Château. By car: Versailles is 21km (13 miles) southwest of Paris by the A13 autoroute; take the exit Versailles-Château. Park on place d'Armes. Handy tip: to avoid queuing, book tickets for the palace in advance via www.chateauversailles.fr or on tel: 01 30 83 78 00. One of the simplest tickets is a 'forfeit', covering both the RER fare and entrance to the château and thus avoiding the queue.

To reach the palace of **Versailles ❶** from central Paris, follow the instructions in the box on the left. A tour of the main sections of the palace and gardens is given here, but first some background on the evolution of the château.

BEGINNINGS

In 1623, Louis XIII, a passionate huntsman, built a lodge near the town of Versailles to the west of Paris, in order to take advantage of the thick forest in the area. In 1631, the king instructed his chief architect, Philibert Le Roy, to upgrade the lodge.

Louis XIV

From 1661–8 further changes were made under the young Louis XIV, who poached architect Louis Le Vau, painter Charles Lebrun and landscape gardener André Le Nôtre from the château of Vaux-le-Vicomte, where Finance Minister, Nicolas Fouquet, had been outdoing the king in splendour and style.

Versailles was still too small, however, for king and entourage, so in 1668 Louis commissioned Le Vau to envelop the existing palace in a new building (the white-stone block that backs on to the gardens). From 1678, Jules Hardouin-Mansart took over as main architect, heralding a period of prolific building.

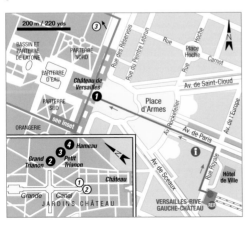

Official Court Residence

In 1682 Versailles became Louis XIV's official residence and the seat of the French government. New construction included the Hall of Mirrors, North and South wings, Stables, Grand Lodgings (staff accommodation), Orangery and Royal Chapel, as well as the redesign of the Grand Trianon.

Upon his proper accession to the throne after the Regency of 1715–22, Louis XV also kept court at Versailles. His architect, Ange-Jacques Gabriel, refurbished the private apartments and built the Petit Trianon (1762–4). Between 1768 and 1770 he also constructed the Royal Opera and in 1771 redesigned Mansart's crumbling North Wing in the classical French style.

REVOLUTION

The court under Louis XVI stayed at Versailles, keeping its distance from the increasingly discontented Parisian mob. This fantasy world was epitomised by the building of the Hameau (hamlet) for Marie-Antoinette between 1783 and 1787. Louis's world collapsed, however, when on 6 October 1789 he and his family were forced to return to the Palais des Tuileries in Paris. Louis, the last king in the Bourbon line, was guillotined on 21 January 1793, in what is now place de la Concorde *(see p.43)*.

NAPOLEON

After the Revolution, the palace was looted, and the estate fell into disrepair. Napoleon considered moving here, after his marriage in 1810 to his second wife, Archduchess Marie-Louise, but the plans never came to fruition. However, the couple did enjoy retreats in the Grand Trianon, and the Emperor gave the Petit Trianon to his sister Pauline.

MUSEUM

Future occupants of the château did little to benefit it. Louis-Philippe of Orléans, who reigned 1830–48, carried out renovation work, but his transformation of parts of the château into a museum 'To all the Glories of France' took its toll on the buildings.

During the late 19th and the 20th century Versailles' main function was as a military headquarters: for the Germans during the Franco-Prussian War, for the Allied War Council during World War I, and then in World War II, from 1944 to 1945, for the Allies.

THE MAIN PALACE

Start the tour at the main palace, which can be visited without a guide. It includes the **Grands Appartements** (State Apartments) of the King and Queen, where the monarch's every move was scrutinised by a league of courtiers.

Here too is the **Galerie des Glaces** (Hall of Mirrors), best visited in the afternoon, when the sun streams in. Seventeen arched windows correspond to 17 mirrored arcades, and the vaulted ceiling features captions from the playwright Racine and 30 paintings by Lebrun of great events from the first 17 years of Louis XIV's 72-year reign.

Above from far left: portrait of Marie-Antoinette; the grand exterior of Versailles; chief painter to the King, Charles le Brun oversaw the painting of the lavish ceilings such as this one.

Control Freak Keeping the court and government at Versailles was an arrangement that enabled Louis XIV, a firm believer in absolute monarchy ('L'Etat c'est moi' – I am the state), to maintain strict control over both the affairs of state and the behaviour of his courtiers.

Above from left: palace ceiling; idyllic Versailles scenery.

It was in this room that the Treaty of Versailles was signed to signify the end of World War I.

For a supplement (these are charged for most 'extras' at Versailles), you can see Louis XIV's private bedroom and the apartments of the Dauphin and Dauphine. Guided tours are offered for the private apartments of Louis XV, Louis XVI, Marie Antoinette, Madame de Pompadour and Madame du Barry, as well as the opera house (inaugurated to mark the marriage of the future Louis XVI and Marie Antoinette and recently renovated) and royal chapel.

A Very Public Way of Life

The Versailles complex was designed to house the entire court and its entourage: some 20,000 people. Leaving their provincial châteaux or Parisian mansions, members of the nobility were obliged to spend years in service at court, at great personal expense, observing an elaborate system of etiquette in order to try to win the king's favour and the lucrative sinecures that went with it. Instead of plotting civil war, nobles fought for the honour of holding the king's shirt when he got out of bed in the morning during the celebrated public *levée*. Similarly, the king's meals were public ceremonies (the food always went cold), and queens even gave birth in full view of courtiers.

TRIANONS AND HAMEAU

The two other main buildings on the estate are the Grand and Petit Trianons, located to the northwest, about 30 minutes on foot from the château. If you do not want to walk, take the mini train that runs regularly from the château, along the Grand Canal and across to the Trianons and back. Bicycles and horse-drawn carriages may also be hired. Marie-Antoinette's Hameau (classed, along with the Petit Trianon, as 'Marie-Antoinette's Estate') is a cluster of thatched cottages, a 10-minute walk to the northeast.

Grand Trianon

The Italianate **Grand Trianon** ❷ was erected by Louis XIV as a miniature palace and haven from public life in the main château. Le Vau's original design of 1670, decorated in blue-and-white Delftware porcelain, was replaced in 1687 with the marble architecture of Hardouin-Mansart that you see today. After being looted during the Revolution, the Grand Trianon was later redecorated in the Empire style for Napoleon and his second wife Marie-Louise. In more recent times, Charles de Gaulle stayed here during his presidency, and ever since, one wing has been reserved for the French Head of State.

Petit Trianon and Hameau

The **Petit Trianon** ❸ was built for Louis XV in the Greek style by Gabriel from 1762 to 1768 as a retreat for the king and his mistresses Madame de Pompadour, and later Madame du

Barry. The gardens here were designed by the scientist and botanist Bernard de Jussieu and later re-landscaped in the rambling English style for Marie-Antoinette, who was given the Petit Trianon on her accession to the throne.

Also linked with Marie Antoinette is the **Hameau** ❹, a cluster of thatched cottages by architect Richard Mique. The official Versailles guidebooks stress that these rustic-style buildings were not erected, as is popularly believed, so that the Queen could play at being a shepherdess, but as a dairy where food for the royal estate was produced.

THE GARDENS AND PARK

The château's 815ha (2,000 acres) of gardens and park are the work of André Le Nôtre, who created the ultimate French playground for Louis XIV out of unpromising hillocks and marshland.

A principal feature of the park is the **Grande Canal** (Grand Canal), an ornamental stretch of water covering 44ha (105 acres), which can be explored by boat. Around the canal, a network of pathways, fountain basins, groves adorned with statuary, and sculpted trees and bushes, radiates out symmetrically. Look out for the **Orangerie**, with a vaulted gallery that could house over 2,000 orange trees, and the Potager du Roi, the king's vegetable garden.

Fountain Displays

Note that there is an extra charge for the gardens on Sundays, when the fountains, powered by an ingenious hydraulic system, come to life and 17th-century music blasts over the *parterres*. However, Sunday is also the day when the château's interior is most crowded.

Eating

Of the cafés and restaurants within the grounds, two of the best are **La Flottille**, see ⓘⓘ, and **La Petite Venise**, see ⓘ②. There are also inexpensive open-air eating areas serving snacks in the groves on either side of the Latona Garden and Royal Avenue. Depending on the weather, the best plan may be to bring a gourmet picnic.

One option is to have a meal at **Gordon Ramsay au Trianon**, see ⓘ③, at the northeastern edge of the palace grounds. From there, walk southeast to return to the station at Versailles.

Food and Drink 🍴

① LA FLOTTILLE
Tel: 01 39 51 41 58; €€
At the head of the Grand Canal is this restaurant (serving standard French fare), brasserie (chicken-and-chips-style food) and *salon de thé*.

② LA PETITE VENISE
Tel: 01 39 53 25 69; €€
Located between the Bassin d'Apollon and the Grand Canal, this venue also functions as a restaurant, brasserie and *salon de thé*.

③ GORDON RAMSAY AU TRIANON
Trianon Palace, 1 boulevard de la Reine, Versailles; tel: 01 30 84 55 55; Tue–Sat 7–10.30pm; €€€€
Set within the Trianon Palace hotel, on the edge of the palace grounds, is Gordon Ramsay's first fine-dining restaurant in France. A smart affair (no jeans or T-shirts).

Additional Sights
Other attractions at Versailles include the Jeu de Paume indoor real-tennis courts, situated just outside the Versailles estate on rue du Jeu de Paume, and Hardouin-Mansart's stables, located below the parade ground, between St-Cloud, Paris and Sceaux avenues. The stables are now home to Versailles' carriage museum.

FONTAINEBLEAU

Louis IX called Fontainebleau his 'wilderness', François I referred to trips here as 'coming home', and, from exile in St Helena, Napoleon Bonaparte called it 'the true home of kings'. Little wonder it is now a World Heritage Site.

Fond Farewell
The main White Horse Courtyard is also known as the Farewell Courtyard. It was from the double-horseshoe staircase that Napoleon took his leave for Elba in 1814 after signing his first act of abdication at Fontainebleau.

DISTANCE 120km (74miles) rtn
TIME A full day
START/END Fontainebleau

Note that the distance above is from central Paris. To reach the palace by train: from the Gare de Lyon to Fontainebleau-Avon (45 mins), then 'Château' bus from the station or 30-min walk through town. Check train times before travelling, at www.sncf. fr, as services are infrequent. SNCF sells an all-in-one train-bus-château ticket. By car: take the Fontainebleau exit on the A6 autoroute; the château is 16km (10 miles) away. Parking is available in the town. Allow at least 2 hours to do the tour of the palace.

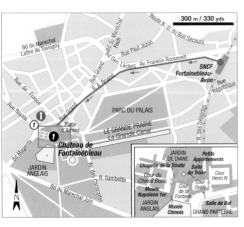

Close to the town centre of Fontaine-bleau is the **Château de Fontainebleau** ❶ (place Général de Gaulle; tel: 01 60 71 50 70; www.musee-chateau-fontaine bleau.fr; Wed–Mon 9.30am–5pm, Apr–Sept till 6pm; charge), the only fully furnished royal palace in France.

BACKGROUND

In 1528, to indulge his passion for blood sports, François I commissioned a palace in the Mannerist style on the site of a medieval royal hunting lodge near the 100-sq km (40-sq mile) Fôret de Fontainebleau. Just back from his conquests in Italy, François introduced to France the Renaissance style, which became known as the First Fontaine-bleau School. He also embellished his palace with paintings by Leonardo da Vinci, including the *Mona Lisa* (now in the Louvre), and Raphael.

Palace Evolution
Renovations and additions were carried out under Henri II, Henri IV, Louis XIV and Louis XVI, but with the latter came the French Revolution, and the palace was no longer the home of kings. It was stripped of its contents and left to ruin, until 1803, when Napoleon founded a military school here and began a full refurbishment.

During the Bourbon Restoration (1815–30), Louis Philippe continued the renovation, followed, in the Second Republic, by Bonaparte's nephew, Napoleon III. In the late 19th century Empress Eugénie added new salons and a Chinese Museum. From 1945 to 1965 the palace was the headquarters of the military branch of Nato.

PALACE TOUR

The entrance is on the right-hand side of the **Cour du Cheval Blanc** (White Horse Courtyard), as you stand facing the double-horseshoe staircase *(see left)*. This is the Louis XV wing, which houses the **Musée Napoléon I**, showcasing clothing, weapons, accessories and paintings relating to the emperor.

First Floor
At the end of this wing, ascend the stairs to the **Grands Appartements** (State Apartments) and Renaissance rooms. Highlights include the Galerie François I, emblazoned with his initials and heraldic salamander, the ballroom and the Salon Louis XIII, in which the future king was born in 1601. Also exceptional is the 80m (262ft) Galerie de Diane, converted in 1858 into a library by Napoleon III, and the king's bedroom, transformed in 1808 into a throne room. Also on the upper floor is Napoleon's elegant Imperial Apartment, decorated in the Empire Style.

Ground Floor
The tour continues on the ground floor, where, immediately to the left of the double-horseshoe staircase, is the 16th-century **Chapelle de la Trinité**, in which Louis XV was married in 1725. Ahead are the modest **Petits Appartements** (Small Apartments; restricted hours), which Napoleon I created as a private suite for himself and his first wife Josephine, although hers was later used by his second wife Marie-Louise.

You can also visit Empress Eugénie's salons and the **Musée Chinois** (Chinese Museum), although both are also open for restricted hours only.

The Garden
Highlights in the grounds include the early 19th-century English garden, the carp pond, the Grand Parterre (the first in this formal French style), the canal and what is still the largest *jeu de paume* (real-tennis court) in the world.

BACK TO TOWN

When you have seen enough of the palace, return to the town by exiting the main gate, crossing place d'Armes and heading along rue du Château (later rue Grande). Our recommendation of where to eat in town is the **François 1er**, see 🍴①.

Food and Drink 🍴
① LE FRANÇOIS 1ER (CHEZ BERNARD)
3 rue Royale, Fontainebleau; tel: 01 64 22 24 68; €€
One of the best restaurants in town with a terrace overlooking the château. Chef Bernard Crogiez's cuisine is especially fine in game season.

Above from far left: Louis XVI wing; the carp pond; statue by the Louis XVI wing.

Vaux-le-Vicomte
You could combine this tour with a visit to the palace at Vaux-le-Vicomte (Maincy; tel: 01 64 14 41 90; www.vaux-le-vicomte.com; end Mar–early Nov 10am–6pm; also for candlelit evenings, see website for details; charge), as the two are within 16km (10 miles) of each other and on the same train line (RER D/mainline train to Melun, then shuttlebus – weekends and public hols only – or taxi). Vaux is the former home of Louis XIV's one-time Finance Minister, Nicolas Fouquet, and generally considered to be the forerunner to Versailles.

GIVERNY

A visit to Monet's house, at Giverny in Normandy, is an exercise in retinal pleasure. Gardens brimming with flowers, a Japanese bridge, waterlilies and a pink house: it's easy to see why he proclaimed it 'a splendid spot for me'.

DISTANCE 160km (100 miles) rtn

TIME A full day

START Fondation Monet

END Musée des Impressionnismes

GETTING TO GIVERNY

To reach the start point by train: from the Gare St-Lazare to Vernon (45 mins) trains are infrequent, so check times in advance (SNCF tel: 36 35 from within France or +33 8 92 35 35 35 from abroad, www.sncf.com); at Vernon take a bus 15 mins to the village (no. 240 leaves the station about 15 mins after the arrival of Paris train); or, rent a bike from opposite the station (€8 per day, 25 mins ride on the flat; see www.fondation-monet.com for details of the route). By car: take the A13 west to Bonnières, then the D201 to Giverny.

Beat the Crowds

Monet's house and garden can be extremely crowded with coach parties and school visits, particularly towards the end of term and during the summer holidays. Try to avoid the masses by aiming for an early morning or late afternoon visit. Despite the crowds, the house and garden are engagingly pretty. You can also buy your ticket online to save queuing time.

Claude Monet (1840–1926) discovered Giverny, where the Seine meets the river Epte, in 1883, spying it from the door of the little train that used to run at the bottom of what is now the Clos Normand garden. He moved here with his own two children, his mistress Alice Heschedé (his wife had died of tuberculosis in 1879) and her six children, and lived here for 43 years until his death.

In the early years, Monet was desperately short of money, and his art dealer, Durand-Ruel, helped him pay the rent. Eventually, though, the painter prospered: he purchased this house, married Alice, and laid out the gardens you see today at great expense.

FONDATION MONET

From the car and coach parks, it is just a hop to 84 rue Claude Monet and the **Fondation Monet ❶** (tel: 02 32 51 28 21, www.fondation-monet.fr; Apr–Oct: daily 9.30am–6pm; charge). After passing through the ticket windows, you reach the museum shop, once one of the many studios that Monet built around the property, and used for the production of the waterlily paintings, *Les Nymphéas*, now in the Musée de l'Orangerie *(see p.35)* in Paris. The shop is well stocked with waterlily-patterned ties and tea towels.

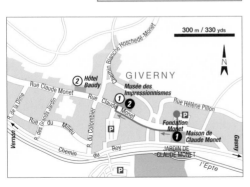

The House

After the shop, on the right, is Monet's eccentrically coloured house: pink and green on the outside, while inside the dining room is bright yellow, and the kitchen is sky blue. Upstairs, the bedrooms are light and airy, with big windows on to the gardens. The walls of the artist's rooms feature Japanese prints from his extensive collection.

The Garden

The garden is already familiar to many from Monet's paintings. Immediately in front of the house is the grid pattern of flowerbeds of the Clos Normand. Below is the Water Garden, for which Monet bought the land in 1893. Obtaining official permission to dig his ponds was a protracted business, but by 1895 Monet was able to have his waterlilies, the Japanese bridge, the willows and the pond with punt. By then, he was in full swing, adding three hothouses for his collections of begonias, exotic ferns and orchids. In 1966, Monet's son Michel bequeathed the property to the state.

MUSÉE DES IMPRESSIONNISMES

When you've seen enough of the gardens, turn left out of the Fondation and walk along rue Claude Monet. At no. 99 is the **Musée des Impressionnismes** ❷ (tel: 02 32 51 94 65; www.museedesimpressionnismesgiverny.com; Apr–Oct: Tue–Sun 10am–6pm; charge), devoted to American artists, who, inspired by the Movement, came to Giverny; see also ⑪①.

Monet was initially receptive to the arrivals, but tired of the invasion: 'When I first came to Giverny I was quite alone, the little village was unspoiled. Now, so many artists, students, flock here, I have often thought of moving away.' As you leave, you may feel some sympathy.

Above from far left: Monet's house; his *Japanese Bridge*, painted from c.1895; Oriental poppy in the Clos Normand; waterlilies in the Water Garden.

Hôtel Baudy
The only hotel in the village, the Baudy was once the scene of the tennis parties, amateur theatricals, and drinking sessions of Giverny's colony of American artists. Apparently, on occasion, it also accommodated such esteemed names as Renoir, Rodin, Sisley and Pissarro. Largely unchanged, it is now a pleasant bistro, with walls lined with some of the less distinguished artworks of its former customers. See also ⑪②.

Food and Drink 🍴

① TERRA CAFÉ
99 rue Claude Monet, Giverny; tel: 02 32 51 94 61; €€
The restaurant of the Musée des Impressionnismes offers salads, quiches, fish and grilled meat, and fine views of the pretty gardens from the terrace. You can eat here without a museum ticket.

② HÔTEL BAUDY
81 rue Claude Monet, Giverny; tel: 02 32 21 10 03; daily 10am–8.30pm; €€
Once the focal point for the village's American artists, this hotel has a restaurant that does classic French food and terrace seating.

Left: the painter in his garden c.1920.

DISNEYLAND PARIS

If your children are tired of art museums, and unimpressed with another lunch of foie gras, then Disneyland Resort Paris may be in order. Here, they can enjoy all the latest fairground rides and as many burgers as they can eat.

Tickets and Times

With some variation, times are: main park Sept–mid-July Mon–Fri 10am–8pm, Sat–Sun 9am–8pm, mid-July–Aug daily 9am–11pm; Walt Disney Studios: summer daily 9am–7pm, winter Mon–Fri 10am–6pm, Sat–Sun 9am–6pm; for bookings and information: tel: 08 25 30 60 30 (France) 08705 030303 (UK) or visit www.disneylandparis.co.uk.

DISTANCE 64km (40 miles) rtn
TIME At least a full day
START/END Disneyland
POINTS TO NOTE

The distance above is from central Paris. Directions on how to get to the park are as follows: by public transport, catch the RER A from central Paris at Auber, Châtelet or Étoile to Disneyland Resort Paris; by car, take the A4 east of Paris to Marne-la-Vallée (exit 14), where there are signs to the resort and car parks. If you are arriving direct from the UK, Eurostar and TGV trains run from London; see www.eurostar.com.

Located on a 83-ha (205-acre) site at Marne-la-Vallée, east of Paris, **Disneyland Resort Paris** ❶ *(for opening times, etc, see left)* covers an area one-fifth of the size of Paris. It welcomed 15.4 million visitors in 2009 – more than any other single attraction in Europe – 48 percent of whom were from France and 14 percent from Britain. Given the amount to see, families might consider spreading a visit over two days. The on-site hotels are costly, but staying on the spot means early access to the attractions. The park's official language is English, but French is widely spoken.

Homecoming

According to the Disney marketing machine, Disneyland Paris was something of a homecoming; Walt's family came from Isigny-sur-Mer in Normandy, and the name d'Isigny (from Isigny) became Disney in the US. But financial governmental incentives, not family history, were behind the final decision to bring Disney to Europe.

The complex has three parts: the main park, Walt Disney Studios (a self-contained park that offers a behind-the-scenes look at the history of animation, film and television) and the hotels and shops of Disney Village.

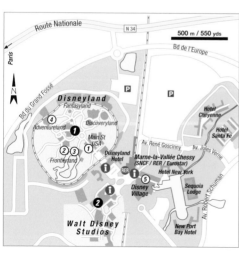

THE MAIN PARK

Disneyland's 'imagineers' have created five 'magic lands': **Fantasyland**, the most popular area for children, with boat trips, carousels and a hedge maze; **Main Street USA**, representing the early 1900s, with ragtime and Dixieland bands (though also featuring Cinderella's Castle); **Frontierland**, evoking the wild west; **Adventureland**, with characters such as Captain Hook; and the futuristic **Discoveryland**, which has a Space Mountain, and French-themed attractions, such as an underwater trip that pays homage to celebrated French sci-fi writer Jules Verne's *20,000 Leagues Under the Sea*.

WALT DISNEY STUDIOS

Disneyland Resort Paris celebrated its 10th anniversary in 2002 by opening up **Walt Disney Studios ❷**, which has four studio lots to entice visitors. Directly through the entrance is **Front Lot**, a mock film set of a street. There's also **Production Courtyard**, giving an insight into the production process; this will be the site of the Studio Tram Tour, a ride that will let you see what it feels like to be slap-bang in the middle of the filming action.

Then there's **Backlot**, which documents stunts and special effects – a great area for older children, teens and adults. And lastly there's **Toon Studio**, which goes back to basics with pen and paper to explain how animated classics are made.

DISNEY VILLAGE

The wider resort, **Disney Village**, is a celebration of 'Americana' and home to the resort hotels. Hotel Cheyenne is the most imaginative: a film-set Western hotel, with saloon, sheriff's jail and wooden-planked stores. Several hotels overlook Lake Disney, including Hotel New York, offering luxury rooms in a Manhattan-style skyscape.

The jewel in the park's crown is the elegant Victorian-style Disneyland Hotel, while in a forest 5km (3 miles) from the main park is Davy Crockett Ranch, where accommodation comprises camping and caravanning places and log cabins, with bike hire available.

Above from far left: a warm welcome from Mickey; Disney Village; Buzz Lightyear and Woody join in the fun.

Food and Drink

The following is just a sample of the dozens of places to eat in Disneyland, most of which get very busy at mealtimes.

① GIBSON GIRL ICE CREAM PARLOUR
Main Street USA, Disneyland Park; €
Ice cream, ice cream and ice cream.

② COWBOY COOKOUT BARBECUE
Frontierland, Disneyland Park; €€
Mock barn serving spare ribs, chicken wings, burgers and fries, with performances of country music as entertainment.

③ MRS WINNER'S HOT DOGS
Frontierland, Disneyland Park; €
Takeaway hot dogs.

④ COLONEL HATHI'S PIZZA OUTPOST
Adventureland, Disneyland Park; €€
Pizza and pasta, animatronic birds in a tree above the dining area, and music from the Disney classic *The Jungle Book*.

⑤ BILLY BOB'S COUNTRY WESTERN SALOON
Disney Village; €€
More for adults than children, this restaurant-bar offers live country music and line dancing on three levels.

DIRECTORY

A user-friendly alphabetical listing of practical information, plus hand-picked hotels and restaurants, clearly organised by area, to suit all budgets and tastes. Select entertainment listings are also included here.

A

ADDRESSES

Paris is divided into 20 numbered districts, called *arrondissements* because they fan out in a 'round' pattern, clockwise from the city centre. Officially they are labelled by a five-digit postcode (75001, 75002, etc), but most people refer to them by their abbreviated form (1st, 2nd, 3rd, 4th, etc).

B

BICYCLES

Some 20,000 bikes in around 1,500 racks across Paris can be used by anyone under the city's pioneering Vélib' (from 'vélo libre' or 'bike for free') scheme: www.velib.paris.fr. Simply swipe your credit card (some US cards may not work) or your Navigo Découverte travel card *(see p.109)*, and pedal away. Depending on your usage, you will be charged either for one or seven days after the first half an hour, which is free.

BUSINESS HOURS

Traditionally, **banks** open from Monday to Friday 9am to 5.30pm and are closed at weekends. However, many now open on Saturday morning and close on Monday instead.

Most **boutiques** and **department stores** open between 9 and 10am, closing at around 7pm (later on Thursday). **Food shops**, especially bakers, open earlier. Lunchtime closing is increasingly rare; most shops do, however, close on Sunday, but bakers and patisseries usually open in the morning.

C

CLIMATE

The average maximum in July and August is 25°C (77°F), the average minimum 15°C (59°F), but 27°C (81°F) is not unusual. In January, expect a maximum of 6°C (43°F), a minimum of 1°C (34°F).

CRIME AND SAFETY

In the event of loss or theft, a report must be made in person at the nearest police station *(commissariat)* as soon as possible. See www.prefecture-police-paris.interieur.gouv.fr for addresses of stations; for emergency help tel: 17.

If you lose your passport, report it to your consulate straight after notifying the police. There is a list of consulates *(consulats)* in the local *Yellow Pages (Pages Jaunes)*, see www. pagesjaunes.fr. **Security**: It is advisable to take the same precautions in Paris as you would in any other capital city, notably watching out for pickpockets on public transport and shielding your PIN at ATM machines. Known centres of prostitution (such as parts of the Bois de Boulogne) are best avoided at night.

CUSTOMS REGULATIONS

Visitors of all nationalities must declare, upon arrival or departure, sums of cash exceeding €10,000 (or equivalent).

Duty-Paid Goods: If you are an EU resident and buy goods in France on which you pay tax, there are no restrictions on the amounts you may take home with you. However, EU law has set 'guidance levels' on the amounts that are acceptable of the following, and if you exceed these amounts you must be able to show that the goods are for personal use:

• Spirits: 10 litres
• Fortified wine/wine: 90 litres (not more than 60 litres may be sparkling)
• Beer: 110 litres.

Duty-Free Goods: If you are from outside the EU and buy goods duty-free in France, the following limits still apply (these quantities may be doubled if you live outside Europe):

• Tobacco: 200 cigarettes, or 100 cigarillos, or 50 cigars, or 250g of tobacco
• Alcohol: 1 litre of spirits/liqueurs over 22 percent volume, or 2 litres under 22 percent. 4 litres still wine and 16 litres beer
• Perfume: 50g of perfume, plus 250ml of eau de toilette.

D

DISABLED TRAVELLERS

French Organisations: Association des Paralysés de France, 17 boulevard Auguste-Blanqui, 13th; tel: 01 40 78 69 00; www.apf.asso.fr.

UK Organisations: RADAR, the Royal Association for Disability and Rehabilitation, 12 City Forum, 250 City Road, London EC1V 8AF; tel: 020-7250 3222; www.radar.org.uk.

US Organisations: Society for Accessible Travel and Hospitality (SATH), 347 Fifth Avenue, Suite 610, New York; tel: 212-447 7284; www.sath.org.

E

ELECTRICITY

You will need an adaptor for most British and US plugs: French sockets have two round holes. Supplies are 230 volt, and US equipment will need a transformer.

EMBASSIES/CONSULATES

Australia: 4 rue Jean-Rey, 15th; tel: 01 40 59 33 00.

Canada: 35 avenue Montaigne, 8th; tel: 01 44 43 29 00.

Republic of Ireland: *Embassy*: 12 avenue Foch, 16th; tel: 01 44 17 67 00.

UK: *Consulate*: 18bis rue d'Anjou, 8th; tel: 01 44 51 31 00.

US: *Embassy*: Consular Section, 4 avenue Gabriel, 1st; tel: 01 43 12 22 22.

EMERGENCY NUMBERS

Ambulance (SAMU): tel: 15
Fire brigade *(pompiers)*: tel: 18
Police *(police secours)*: tel: 17
From a mobile phone: tel: 112

G

GAY TRAVELLERS

Although France has some way to go before gays have the same rights as heterosexuals, gays and lesbians are

Above from far left: place de la Concorde; tiles at Bastille metro.

Clothing
Paris is a great city to explore on foot, so comfortable walking shoes are essential. Bring warm clothes if you're visiting in winter, as the weather can be very chilly, and remember to have something waterproof (or at least an umbrella) with you in spring or autumn, as showers are quite common.

Gay/Lesbian Literature
There are various free magazines you can pick up in gay bars in the 3rd and 4th *arrondissements*. The magazine *Têtu* (www.tetu.com) is a useful source of information for the gay community, and can be bought at most news kiosks in the city.

increasingly accepted in Paris, and this greater openness is being championed by the city's openly gay mayor Bertrand Delanoë. The Marais (4th *arrondissement*) is the most gay-friendly district. The **Centre Gai et Lesbien**: (63 rue Beaubourg, 3rd; tel: 01 43 57 21 47; www.cglparis.org) houses a lending library and advises on health, social and legal issues.

H

HEALTH

EU Nationals: If you are an EU national and you fall ill in France, you can receive emergency medical treatment from doctors, dentists and hospitals. You will have to pay the cost of this treatment, but are entitled to claim back up to 70 percent if you have a **European Health Insurance Card** (in the UK. tel: 0845-605 0707; www.ehic.org.uk).

North Americans: The International Association for Medical Assistance to Travellers (2162 Gordon Street, Ontario N1L 1G67, Canada; tel: 519-836 0102) is a non-profit-making group that offers members fixed rates for medical treatment, a medical record from their doctor and a directory of English-speaking doctors in France. Free membership.

American Hospital (Hôpital Américain de Paris): 63 boulevard Victor Hugo, Neuilly; tel: 01 46 41 25 25; www.american-hospital.org; metro: Porte Maillot, then bus 82 to the last stop. Private hospital with English-speaking staff.

Pharmacies
Most pharmacies are open from 9 or 10am to 7 or 8pm. At night, they post the addresses of the nearest late-opening pharmacies in their windows. Late-opening pharmacies include **Publicis Drugstore**, 133 avenue des Champs-Élysées, 8th; tel: 01 44 43 75 07; Mon–Fri 8am–2am, Sat–Sun 10am–2am; metro: Charles de Gaulle-Étoile.

L

LOST PROPERTY

To reclaim lost items in Paris, go in person (with ID) to the Bureau des Objets Trouvés, 36 rue des Morillons, 15th; tel: 08 21 00 25 25; Mon–Thur 8.30am–5pm, Fri 8.30am–4.30pm; metro: Convention.

M

MEDIA

Newspapers: The two main national dailies are *Le Monde*, which has a rather dry and leftish slant, and the more conservative *Le Figaro*. On the far left is the Communist *L'Humanité*, while between that and *Le Monde* is Jean-Paul Sartre's brainchild, *Libération*. France's biggest-selling daily is the evening paper *France-Soir*.

The major weekly news magazines are *Le Point* (right), *L'Express* (centre) and *Le Nouvel Observateur* (left).

To find out what is going on in Paris, buy *L'Officiel des Spectacles* (out on Wednesday), with listings of films, clubs,

Maps
Paris Classique par Arrondissement is similar to the London *A–Z* and can be bought for about €10 at newsstands.

exhibitions, concerts, theatres etc.

Radio: France Inter (87.8 MHz) is the biggest station, offering something to suit all tastes. Radio Classique (101.1 MHz) plays lightweight classical music. For something slightly less mainstream, try France Musiques (91.7 and 92.1 MHz), or RTL (104.3 MHz), which plays chart music interspersed with chat. Europe 1 (104.7 FM) is the best for morning news coverage, while France Info (105.5 FM) broadcasts the news.

Television: TF1, France 2, France 3, France 5/Arte and M6 are the five main television stations. There is also a huge choice of cable channels. Canal+ is a subscription channel, which shows big-name films.

MONEY

Currency: France uses the euro, divided into 100 cents. Coins *(pièces)* come in 1, 2, 5, 10, 20 and 50 cents, and 1 and 2 euros. Banknotes *(billets)* come in 5, 10, 20, 50, 100, 200 and 500 euros.

Public Holidays

1 Jan (New Year's Day)

Mar/Apr (Easter Monday)

1 May (Labour Day)

8 May (end of World War II in Europe)

Mid-/late May (Ascension Day)

Late May (Whit Monday)

14 July (Bastille Day)

15 Aug (Feast of the Assumption)

1 Nov (All Saints' Day)

11 Nov (Armistice Day, 1918)

25 Dec (Christmas)

Cash Machines: The easiest way to take out money is to use an ATM, with a debit or credit card such as Visa, MasterCard, Maestro or Cirrus, etc, and your PIN.

Credit Cards: Most shops, restaurants and hotels accept credit cards.

POST

Post Offices: Main branches are open Mon–Fri 8am–7pm, Sat 8am–noon. The central post office is at 52 rue du Louvre, 1st; www.laposte.fr.

RELIGION

The majority of people in Paris are nominally Roman Catholic. The *Yellow Pages (Les Pages Jaunes)*, see www. pages jaunes.fr, lists places of worship for every faith and denomination.

T

TELEPHONES

Phone Numbers: All telephone numbers in France have 10 digits. Paris and Île-de-France (Paris region) landline numbers begin with 01. Toll-free telephone numbers start 0800; all other numbers beginning 08 (accessible in France only) are charged at variable rates; 06 numbers are for mobile phones. For the operator, call 12.

Above from far left: metro sign; Paris newsstand.

Green Issues
For information on environmental matters in Paris, visit the news section of www.environnement. paris.fr. When throwing away litter, note that white-lidded bins are for glass, yellow-lidded ones are for everything else recyclable and green bins are for non-recyclable rubbish.

Calling from Abroad: To dial Paris from the UK: 00 (international code) + 33 (France) + 1 (Paris) + an eight-figure number. To call other countries from France, dial the international code (00), then the country code: Australia 61, UK 44, US and Canada 1.

If using a US credit phonecard, call the company's access number: **Sprint**, tel: 08 00 99 00 87; **AT&T**, tel: 08 00 99 00 11; **MCI**, tel: 08 00 99 00 19.

Public Telephone Boxes: Most phone boxes in Paris are operated with a card *(télécarte)*, bought from kiosks, *tabacs* and post offices. Cafés and *tabacs* often have public phones, which usually take coins or *jetons*, discs bought at the bar.

TIME ZONES

France is one hour ahead of Greenwich Mean Time (GMT) and six ahead of Eastern Standard Time.

TOUR OPERATORS

By Boat: Seine cruises last an hour, with commentaries in several languages. In high season, boats leave every half-hour, 10am–10pm. **Batobus** is a 'riverbus' service based at Port de la Bourdonnais by the Eiffel Tower (tel: 08 25 05 01 01; www.batobus.com). **Bateaux Mouches** depart from Pont de l'Alma (tel: 01 42 25 96 10; www.bateaux-mouches.fr); **Vedettes du Pont Neuf** depart from Pont Neuf (tel: 01 46 33 98 38; www.vedettesdupontneuf.com). **Canal Trips**: These run along the Canal St-Martin, from the Bastille to the Parc de la Villette and vice versa.

Try **Canauxrama** (13 quai de la Loire, 19th; tel: 01 42 39 15 00; www.canauxrama.com) or **Paris Canal** (19–21 quai de la Loire, 19th; tel: 01 42 40 96 97; www.pariscanal.com).

By Coach: Most companies provide a commentary in several languages and pass the major sights, but do not stop along the way. **Les Cars Rouges** (English and French; tel: 01 53 95 39 53; www.carsrouges.com) runs double-decker buses to the main tourist sites. Hop off, sightsee, then catch a later bus. **Paris L'Open Tour** (tel: 01 42 66 56 56; www.paris-cityrama.com), operated by RATP, runs a similar service, also with open-topped double-decker buses.

By 2CV: **4 Roues sous 1 Parapluie** (22 rue Bernard, Dimey, 18th; tel: 0800 800 631 (free) or 06 67 32 26 68; www.4roues-sous-1parapluie.com) offers tours of the city in a soft-topped Citroën 2CV (hence the name: four wheels under an umbrella). Each car holds a maximum of three passengers.

TOURIST INFORMATION

In Paris: see http://en.parisinfo.com for details of all services. To call the Paris Tourist Office, tel: 08 92 68 30 00; calls cost €0.34 per minute. Branches include:

• **Main Branch**: 25 rue des Pyramides, 1st; Mon–Sat 10am–7pm, Sun 11am–7pm; metro: Pyramides.

• **Gare de Lyon**, 20 boulevard Diderot, 12th; Mon–Sat 8am–6pm; metro: Gare de Lyon.

• **Gare du Nord**, 18 rue de Dunkerque, 10th; daily 8am–6pm; metro: Gare du Nord.

• **Montmartre**, 21 place du Tertre, 18th; daily 10am–7pm; metro: Abbesses.

UK: Lincoln House, 300 High Holborn, London WC1V 7JH; tel: 0906 824 4123 (60p per min); http://uk.franceguide.com; Mon–Fri 10am–6pm, Sat 10am–4pm.

US: Enquiries via email at info.us @franceguide.com; see also http://us.franceguide.com.

TRANSPORT

Arrival

By Rail: Eurostar has fast, frequent rail services from London (St Pancras) or Ashford station to Paris (Gare du Nord). The service runs about 12 times a day and takes just over two hours (two hours from Ashford). For reservations, tel: 08432-186 186 (UK) or 08 92 35 35 39 (France) or visit www.eurostar.com. There are reduced fares for children aged 4–11; under 4s travel free but are not guaranteed a seat.

By Sea: Ferries running from the UK to northern France offer attractive prices in competition with the Channel Tunnel. There are motorway links from Boulogne, Calais and Le Havre to Paris.

By Air: Air France KLM is the main agent for flights to France from the US and within Europe. For British travellers, in addition to major airlines (British Airways, etc), the low-cost airlines easyJet and bmi offer flights to Paris from London and/or other British cities. Ryanair fly between Paris Beauvais and Glasgow and Dublin.

By Car: Eurotunnel takes cars from Folkestone to Calais on the drive-on, drive-off **Le Shuttle**. It takes 35 minutes from platform to platform and about one hour from motorway to motorway. Payment is made at toll booths, which accept cash, cheques or credit cards. The price applies to the car, not the number of passengers.

You can book in advance with Eurotunnel on tel: 08443-353 535 (UK) or 08 10 63 03 04 (France) or at www.eurotunnel.com. You can also just turn up and take the next available service. Le Shuttle runs 24 hours a day, and there are from two to five an hour, depending on the season and time.

By Bus: National Express Eurolines runs services daily from London's Victoria Coach Station to Paris, providing one of the cheaper ways to get there. Discounts are available for young people and senior citizens, and the ticket includes the ferry crossing. For details tel: 08717-818181; www.nationalexpress.com; or Eurolines France, at the Gare Routière-Coach Station Galliéni, 28 avenue du Général de Gaulle, Bagnolet; tel: 08 92 89 90 91; metro Galliéni. See also www.eurolines.fr.

Airports

• **Roissy-Charles-de-Gaulle**: The fastest way of getting to central Paris from Roissy-Charles-de-Gaulle is by RER train. These leave every 15 minutes between around 5am and 11.45pm from terminal 2 and run to the metro at Gare du Nord or Châtelet. The journey takes around 45 minutes.

The **Roissy** bus runs between the airport and rue Scribe (near the Palais-Garnier) from terminals 1, 2 and 3. It

Above from far left: gridlock at the Arc de Triomphe.

Stamps

These *(timbres)* are available at most *tabacs* (tobacconists) and other shops selling postcards or greetings cards. For more details and postage costs, visit www.laposte.fr.

runs every 15 minutes 8am–8.45pm, then every 30 minutes until 11pm. From the Palais-Garnier it runs from 5.45am–11pm, every 15–30 minutes. The **Air France bus** (to metro Porte de Maillot or Charles-de-Gaulle Étoile) runs every 15 minutes from 5.40am to 11pm.

By **taxi**, the journey from Charles de Gaulle can take anything from around 30 minutes to over an hour, depending on the traffic. The charge is metered, with supplements payable for each large piece of luggage. An average fare between the airport and central Paris is €40 by day, €50 at night.

• **Orly**: To get to central Paris from Orly, take the **shuttle** from Orly Sud or Orly Ouest to Orly railway station. The RER stops at Austerlitz, Pont St-Michel and the Quai d'Orsay. It runs every 15 minutes from 5.50am to 10.50pm and takes around 30 minutes to Austerlitz.

Alternatively, the **Orlybus** (to place Denfert-Rochereau) leaves from Orly Sud or Orly Ouest. It runs every 15–20 minutes from 6am to 11.30pm. The costlier **Orlyval** automatic train is a shuttle to Antony (the nearest RER to Orly). It runs every 4–7 minutes, 6am–11pm, and takes 35 minutes.

Air France buses (to Invalides, Etoile and Gare Montparnasse) leave from Orly Sud or Orly Ouest. They run every 20 minutes from 6am to 11pm and take 30 minutes. Tickets are available from the Air France terminus. See also www.carsairfrance.com.

By **taxi**, the journey from Orly to the city centre takes around 20–40 minutes, depending on the traffic.

Transport within Paris

Bus *(autobus)*: Bus transport around Paris is efficient, though not always fast. You can get a bus map from metro station ticket offices. Most buses run 7am–8.30pm, some until 12.30am. Service is reduced on Sundays and public holidays. Some 47 Noctilien lines run from 12.30am–5.30am, with hubs at the Gare de l'Est, Gare Montparnasse, Gare St-Lazare, Châtelet and Gare de Lyon.

Tickets: You can buy a ticket as you board, but it's cheaper to buy a book of tickets *(carnet)* from any metro station or tobacconist. Bus and metro tickets are interchangeable. Punch your ticket in the validating machine when you get on. You can also buy special Paris Visite tourist passes or a Navigo Découverte swipe card *(see opposite)*.

Metro: The Paris Métropolitain is one of the most efficient and least expensive metro systems in the world. Services start at about 5.30am and finish around 1am. The RATP (metro organisation) has an information office at 54 quai de la Rapée, 12th; tel: 32 46 (within France); www.ratp.fr.

Express lines (RER – Réseau Express Régional) get you into the centre of Paris from the suburbs in about 15 minutes, with a few stops in between.

You can buy single tickets or you can get 10 journeys for the price of seven with a *carnet* (book) of tickets, also valid for the bus network and for the RER, provided that you stay within Paris and don't go to outer suburbs.

A **Paris Visite** ticket, valid for one, two, three or five days, for 1–3 or 1–6 zones (the latter includes airport links

and travel to Disneyland Resort Paris and Versailles), allows unlimited travel on the bus, suburban trains, RER, trams or metro, and reductions on entrance fees to various attractions. A day ticket, **Forfait 1 Jour Mobilis**, is valid for the metro, RER, buses, suburban trains and some airport buses.

For longer stays, the best buy is a **Navigo Découverte** swipe card. It costs €5 for the card itself (and you'll need a passport photograph), which can then be topped up to make it into either a weekly *(hebdomadaire)* Mon–Sun, or monthly *(mensuel)* card – the latter dates from the first of the month. The Navigo card allows unlimited rides inside Paris on the metro, RER, suburban train, trams and buses.

Train: The SNCF (French Railways Authority) runs fast, comfortable trains on an efficient network. The high-speed service (TGV – *train à grande vitesse*). See www.sncf.com or www.voyages-sncf.com; tel: 08 92 35 35 35.

Taxi: An unoccupied cab can be recognised by an illuminated white sign on its roof. Fares differ according to the zones covered or the time of the day (you'll be charged more between 5pm and 7am and on Sunday), and there are extra charges for putting luggage in the boot and for pick-up at a station or airport. Taxi drivers can refuse to carry more than three passengers. The fourth, if admitted, pays a supplement.

The following taxi companies take phone bookings 24 hours a day:
- **Alpha**: 01 45 85 85 85
- **G7**: 01 47 39 47 39
- **Taxis Bleus**: 08 91 70 10 10.

Car Rental

To hire a car you will need to show your driving licence (held for at least a year) and passport. You will also need a major credit card, or a large deposit. The minimum age for renting cars is 21, although a young driver's supplement is usually payable for those under 25. Third-party insurance is compulsory, and full cover is recommended.

The international car-hire firms operating in Paris include: **Avis** (tel: 08 21 23 07 60; www.avis.fr), **Europcar/National/InterRent** (tel: 08 25 35 83 58; www.europcar.fr) and **Hertz** (tel: 01 39 38 38 38; www. hertz.fr).

Parking: Street parking is hard to find; spaces are usually controlled until 7pm by pay-and-display machines *(horodateurs)*. Most car parks are underground (visit www.parkingsdeparis.fr).

Petrol (Gas): This can be hard to track down in the city centre, so if your tank is almost empty head for a *porte* (exit) on the Périphérique (the multi-lane ring road), where there are stations open 24 hours a day all year round.

V

VISAS

All visitors to France require a valid passport. No visa is required by visitors from the EU, the US, Australia, Canada, New Zealand or South Africa. Nationals of other countries may need a visa; if in doubt (and, advisably, if visiting for over 90 days), check with the French Consulate in your home country.

Above from far left: on the platform; metro busker.

Paris has the second-largest number of hotel rooms in Europe (after London), with hotels ranging from the pint-sized to the palatial. Most hotels in the centre are concentrated in the 8th *arrondissement* (around the Champs-Élysées), the 9th (around the Opéra and Grand Magasins) and in the 10th (near the Gare du Nord). There are few hotels in the budget range – most are in the two- and three-star category. Don't expect to find a bargain – in general, it's hard to find anything really good, with its own bathroom, for less than 100 euros. In the middle range, the stress is generally on style and charm rather than high-tech facilities. Cheaper options include staying in a B&B *(see margin tip, p.114)*.

The Islands

Henri IV

25 place Dauphine, 1st; tel: 01 43 54 44 53; http://henri4hotel.fr; metro: Pont Neuf; €

Some of the least expensive rooms in Paris can be found at this modest hotel which has been popular with visitors on a budget for decades. The 21 rooms are somewhat old-fashioned, with shared bathrooms, but this pales into insignificance beside the fabulous location on place Dauphine, only a short walk away from Notre-Dame and St-Michel. Reserve well in advance. No credit cards.

Hôtel du Jeu de Paume

54 rue St-Louis-en-l'Ile, 4th; tel: 01 43 26 14 18; www.jeudepaumehotel. com; metro: Pont Marie; €€€–€€€€

Delightfully set on the pretty Île St-Louis, this hotel, with ancient beams and romantic vintage decor, is great for a taste of old Paris. Breakfast is served in the mansion's 17th-century real-tennis court (hence the name). Gym, sauna, library, billiards room, music room, Wi-fi access, concierge and room service.

Louvre, Tuileries and Concorde

Hôtel Costes

239 rue St-Honoré, 1st; tel: 01 42 44 50 00; www.hotelcostes.com; metro: Tuileries; €€€€

This hip hotel is just off elegant place Vendôme in an exclusive neighbourhood lined with chic boutiques. The rooms are exquisitely decorated with Baroque paintings, heavy drapes and antiques. Some bathrooms have claw-foot bathtubs and mosaic tiles. The hallways are lit with candles; even the indoor pool, which has an underwater sound system, is dark. Other facilities include a bar, gym, restaurant, the fashionable Café Costes, room service and parking.

Hôtel de Crillon

10 place de la Concorde, 8th; tel: 01 44 71 15 00; www.crillon.com; metro: Concorde; €€€€

Price for a double room for one night without breakfast:	
€€€€	over 350 euros
€€€	200–350 euros
€€	120–200 euros
€	below 120 euros

This palatial world-renowned hotel forms part of the splendid neoclassical facade that dominates the north side of place de la Concorde. Known for its impeccable service (only to be expected at this price), it also has a legendary bar and two notable restaurants: Michelin-starred Les Ambassadeurs (headed by chef Christopher Hache) and the lighter, more affordable L'Obé. There's also the romantic Winter Garden for tea, coffee and cocktails. In the bedrooms, the decor is fittingly grand. Facilities include a gym, parking and room service.

Opéra and Grands Boulevards

Banke Hotel

20 rue La Fayette, 9th; tel: 01 55 33 22 22; www.hotelbankeparis.com; metro: Chuassée d'Antin – La Fayatte, Gare St-Lazare; €€€

Located in the heart of the Grands Boulevards, in the imposing Hauss-mannian former headquarters of the Crédit Commercial de France (CCF) bank, this hotel screams luxury and comfort, right from the vast domed reception area. There are 94 sound-proofed rooms, which are richly decorated in chocolates, purples, reds and creams, reminiscent of a gentleman's club, with highlights of gold; those on the 6th floor have views of the Sacré-Coeur and the Palais-Garnier. Facilities include several restaurants (including the Josefin, which offers Mediterranean dishes), a bar, gym and spa. There's even a private art collection.

Hôtel Chopin

10 boulevard Montmartre (46 passage Jouffroy), 9th; tel: 01 47 70 58 10; www.hotel-chopin.com; metro: Richelieu Drouot; €

Tucked away at the end of an historic 19th-century glass-and-steel-roofed arcade *(see p.45)*, this is a quiet, friendly and simply furnished hotel, offering 36 rooms at a fabulous price for the location. Facilities are basic, but there are televisions in the rooms, and they are en suite. Book well in advance.

Four Seasons George V

31 avenue George V, 8th; tel: 01 49 52 70 00; www.fourseasons.com/paris; metro: George V, Alma Marceau; €€€€

One of the most famous hotels in Paris, just off the Champs-Élysées. The George V offers the height of opulence, with beautifully decorated, traditional-style rooms with modern touches and magnificent marble bathrooms. Facilities include a fabulous spa inspired by the palace at Versailles, a bar, two restaurants, including the Michelin-starred Le Cinq, and a business centre. Exquisite service.

Hôtel Plaza Athénée

25 avenue Montaigne, 8th; tel: 01 53 67 66 65; www.plaza-athenee-paris.com; metro: Alma Marceau; €€€€

This palatial hotel, with lavish mostly Louis XVI- or Regency-style decor, has sound-proofed rooms, a club, gym, 'Dior Institut' spa and an eponymous restaurant headed by super-chef Alain

Prices and Booking
Hotel prices in Paris are not subject to restrictions and can be changed without notice, so check before booking. The majority of hotels vary prices by season. State your arrival time if you book by phone, or your room will not be held after 7pm.

Ducasse. If you can't stretch to the price of a room, treat yourself to a cocktail in the fashionable bar.

Ritz
15 place Vendôme, 1st; tel: 01 43 16 30 30; www.ritzparis.com; metro: Concorde, Opéra; €€€€

One of the most prestigious addresses in the world, the Ritz has welcomed the most discriminating of guests, including Coco Chanel (who lived in a suite here for 37 years), the Duke and Duchess of Windsor, and Princess Diana and Dodi Al Fayed. Rooms are plush, decorated in Louis XV style with antique clocks and rich tapestries. The spa has a beautiful indoor pool, and there are two fine restaurants, including Michelin-starred L'Espadon, and a pleasant garden. All the facilities one would expect, including a gym and business centre.

Marais and Bastille

Hôtel Caron de Beaumarchais
12 rue du Vieille du Temple, 4th; tel: 01 42 72 34 12; www.caron debeaumarchais.com; metro: St-Paul, Hôtel de Ville; €€

A gorgeous little hotel in an excellent location in one of the nicest streets in the Marais. Rooms are decorated in the romantic French 18th-century style with pretty chandeliers and antiques, in honour of the 18th-century playwright after whom the hotel is named. Very friendly management. There are only 19 rooms, so book in advance.

Hôtel Duo
11 rue du Temple, 4th; tel: 01 42 72 72 22; www.duoparis.com; metro: Hôtel de Ville; €€€

Trendy hotel in a great spot in the Marais, just steps from the Hôtel de Ville. The 58 rooms, which are quiet despite the central location, thanks to excellent sound-proofing, are furnished in contemporary style, with good-sized bathrooms (unusual in Paris). Facilities include a bar, gym, sauna and Wi-fi internet access.

Pavillon de la Reine
28 place des Vosges, 3rd; tel: 01 40 29 19 19; www.pavillon-de-la-reine.com; metro: St Paul; €€€€

This romantic mid-sized hotel, located on the elegant place des Vosges, feels like a chic country château. Rooms vary greatly in size and price, but most have four-poster beds, exposed wooden beams and antiques. There's also a cosy lobby bar with evening wine tasting, and manicured gardens, plus the recently opened Spa de la Reine, with fitness room, jacuzzi, treatment booths and steam room.

Hôtel de la Place des Vosges
12 rue de Birague, 4th; tel: 01 42 72 60 46; www.hotelplacedesvosges. com; metro: St Paul; €–€€

	Price for a double room for one night without breakfast:
€€€€	over 350 euros
€€€	200–350 euros
€€	120–200 euros
€	below 120 euros

An intimate hotel with only 16 rooms in a former stables. It's popular and in a great location by the place des Vosges, so book ahead. A successful marriage of old and new, although still slightly crumbly. Friendly staff.

Hôtel St-Merry

78 rue de la Verrerie, 4th; tel: 01 42 78 14 15; www.hotelmarais.com; metro: Hôtel de Ville; €€–€€€

Arguably the most original hotel in Paris, the St-Merry was once a 17th-century presbytery and is now something of a Gothic masterpiece. The 11 rooms and one suite have stained-glass windows and are decorated with mahogany church pews and iron candelabra and, in one, a carved-stone flying buttress. The phone booth is in a confessional. However, note that high-tech touches are limited here – only the suite has a television, for example.

Champs-Élysées, Trocadéro and West

Hôtel Daniel

8 rue Frédéric Bastiat, 8th; tel: 01 42 56 17 00; www.hoteldanielparis.com; metro: St-Philippe du-Roule, Franklin D. Roosevelt; €€€

A member of the prestigious Relais & Châteaux group, the upmarket Hôtel Daniel is wonderfully romantic, with rooms exquisitely decorated with chinoiserie wallpaper, plush carpets and pretty antiques. Facilities include a bar, restaurant, Wi-fi internet access, parking and room service. An excellent location for the Champs-Élysées and rue du Faubourg St-Honoré.

Montmartre and Pigalle

Hôtel Amour

8 rue Navarin, 9th; tel: 01 48 78 31 80; www.hotelamourparis.fr; metro: St-Georges; €€–€€€

Trendy boutique hotel in the style of an exclusive English gentleman's club, with 20 rooms decorated by contemporary artists; some of them even feature art installations. The bar has DJs, and the pretty restaurant has a garden out the back. Well priced.

Kube Rooms & Bar

1–5 passage Ruelle, 18th; tel: 01 42 05 20 00; www.muranoresort.com; metro: La Chapelle; €€€–€€€€

An achingly trendy designer hotel with a vodka bar in the multicultural Goutte d'Or district. Things are high-tech here: each of the 41 rooms is equipped with a computer with which guests control facilities in their rooms; even opening the doors is activated digitally, by fingertip recognition. Facilities include a gym, Wi-fi internet access, two state-of-the-art screening rooms, a lounge/bar/restaurant, parking and room service.

The East and Northeast

Le Général

5–7 rue Rampon, 11th; tel: 01 47 00 41 57; www.legeneralhotel.com; metro: République; €€

This hotel offers the boutique experience at reasonable prices. The rooms are beautifully decorated, minimalist yet cosy. There's a gym, a sauna and a bar. Room service is available 24/7, and there's Wi-fi internet access too.

Above from far left: intimate decor; exotic blooms; ready for bed; ethnic style.

Point to Note
Not all properties are wheelchair-accessible; even if a hotel does have an elevator, for example, it is likely that it will be a fairly small one. Travellers with disabilities should check before reserving.

The Latin Quarter and St-Germain

Abbaye St-Germain

10 rue Cassette, 6th; tel: 01 45 44 38 11; www.hotelabbayeparis.com; metro: St-Sulpice; €€€

This 17th-century abbey is excellently situated between the Jardin du Luxembourg and St-Germain-des-Prés, and has been sensitively converted into a hotel. The old-style decor, such as the beams and wood panelling, is charming, but there are all modern conveniences, too. Breakfast is served in the garden in summer by attentive staff. Facilities include Wi-fi internet access, room service and a bar.

D'Angleterre

44 rue Jacob, 6th; tel: 01 42 60 34 72; www.hotel-dangleterre.com; metro: St-Germain, Rue du Bac; €€€

This delightful hotel was the site on which the Treaty of Paris, proclaiming the independence of the US, was prepared in 1783; during the 19th century it was used as the British Embassy. Ernest Hemingway lodged here (in room 14) in 1921. The rooms are fairly small and furnished with antiques; only the top-floor doubles are spacious. There's a lovely terrace and garden, where breakfast is served in summer.

Price for a double room for one night without breakfast:	
€€€€	over 350 euros
€€€	200–350 euros
€€	120–200 euros
€	below 120 euros

Hotel des Deux Degrés

10 rue des Grands-Degrés, 5th; tel: 01 55 42 88 88; http://lesdegres hotel.monsite.wanadoo.fr; metro: St-Michel; €€

Romantically furnished hotel in a fabulous location overlooking Notre-Dame (rooms 47 and 501 have views of the cathedral). The 10 rooms are exquisitely decorated with pretty antiques; original wooden beams add to the character. Book well in advance.

Hôtel Esmeralda

4 rue St-Julien-le-Pauvre, 5th; tel: 01 43 54 19 20; metro: St-Michel, Maubert Mutualité; €

The 17th-century Esmeralda, the ultimate in shabby chic, is one of those places you either love or loathe. Its 19 rooms have loud floral wallpaper (probably peeling off the walls), antique furniture (some say 'flea-ridden') and a rickety old staircase (no elevator) that takes some negotiating with suitcases. In addition to the extremely low prices (rooms from around 40 euros for a single) and the undeniable character, the attraction is the incredible location; just under half of the rooms have views of Notre-Dame directly across the Seine.

Hôtel de Nesle

7 rue de Nesle, 6th; tel: 01 43 54 62 41; www.hoteldenesleparis.com; metro: Odéon; €

A laid-back student and backpackers' hotel. Facilities are basic, but the 20 rooms (nine are en suite) are cheerfully decorated with murals, furnished according to eclectic themes

and spotless. There is a garden with a pond, and a hammam.

Hôtel Le Sainte-Beuve

9 rue Ste-Beuve, 6th; tel: 01 45 48 20 07; www.hotel-sainte-beuve.fr; metro: Vavin; €€

The stylish, middle-range Sainte-Beuve, decorated by the British interior designer David Hicks, is set on a quiet street, steps from the excellent shops on rue d'Assas and a short walk from the Jardin du Luxembourg. The rooms are tastefully furnished, with air conditioning; those on the top floor have skylights in the bathrooms and romantic views over the rooftops.

Hôtel Lenox

9 rue de l'Université, 7th; tel: 01 42 96 10 95; www.hotelparislenoxsaint germain.com; metro: St-Germain-des-Prés; €€

This trendy hotel on a quiet road in the up-market 7th *arrondissement* is decorated in classic modern style and is very popular among style-conscious creative types. The 34 recently renovated rooms are spotless, in warm chocolate and raspberry tones. Amenities include a bar, room service and Wi-fi internet.

Hôtel de Verneuil

8 rue de Verneuil, 7th; tel: 01 42 60 82 14; www.hotelverneuil.com; metro: St-Germain; €€–€€€

A cosy characterful hotel in an elegant 17th-century building in the up-market 7th *arrondissement*, with small but attractive rooms in the traditional style and discreet service. Singer Serge Gainsbourg lived just opposite, and the wall outside his old house is decorated with graffiti in homage. Well placed for St-Germain. Wi-fi is available, if you purchase a card from reception.

Hôtel Aviatic

105 rue de Vaugirard; tel: 01 53 63 25 50; www.aviatichotel.com; metro: St-Placide; €€–€€€€

An unpretentious little hotel on a quiet, pleasant street not far from the Jardin du Luxembourg. The comfortable bedrooms have been refurbished, and there is a charming breakfast room decorated with posters, and an elegant Empire-style lounge. Worth upgrading to a superior room, if your budget allows.

Mama Shelter

109 rue de Bagnolet, 20th; tel: 01 43 48 48 48; www.mamashelter.com; metro: Gambetta, Porte de Bagnolet; €–€€€

Located slightly off the beaten track, just east of Père-Lachaise cemetery, this Philippe Starck-designed hotel is billed as a 'sensual refuge'. It's large (172 rooms) and industrial in style, but the biggest surprise is the price, with rooms from around 80 euros, meaning that you really can get design on a budget. Rooms are stylish and contemporary with their own entertainment systems. Facilities include a restaurant, a pizzeria, two chic bars and a shop selling such indispensable items as toothbrushes, phone chargers, etc. Genius.

Above from far left: Canal St-Martin; place St-Germain-des-Prés.

France's dedication to the gastronomic arts is legendary, and the respect for food in all its forms is still strongly in evidence in the capital. Granted, it may not be as cheap as it once was to dine out here – even the classic set menus can seem pricey these days – but that doesn't seem to have deterred either Parisians or tourists. The city is peppered with great eateries, from bistros, brasseries and glitzy Michelin-starred restaurants to Breton crêperies and Moroccan couscouseries and top-notch Asian restaurants, all of which affords plenty of opportunity to sample life as a true *bon viveur*. Note that in up-market restaurants there is often a dress code, with a jacket requested and tie preferred for men. Note, too, that many restaurants close on Sunday evening (brasseries are the useful exception to this) and for the whole of August.

The Islands

L'Escale

1 rue des Deux-Ponts, 4th; tel: 01 43 54 94 23; Mon–Sat nonstop; metro: Pont-Marie; €€

This old-fashioned and pleasantly bustling brasserie-cum-wine bar serves tasty, heartening dishes such as leek quiches, *chou farci* (stuffed cabbage) and *clafoutis* (fruit-and-batter pudding). The wines are well chosen and affordable, and the delicious chips are considerably better than the average brasserie *frite*.

Louvre, Tuileries and Concorde

Le Grand Véfour

17 rue de Beaujolais, 1st; tel: 01 42 96 56 27; www.grand-vefour.com; closed Fri eve, Sat–Sun and Aug; metro: Palais-Royal; €€€€

Hiding under the arches of the Palais-Royal is one of the most beautiful restaurants in Paris. Le Grand Véfour opened its doors in 1784 and has fed the likes of Emperor Napoleon and writers Alphonse Lamartine, Colette, and Victor Hugo. Today it serves haute cuisine under the aegis of chef Guy Martin.

Le Meurice

Hôtel Meurice, 228 rue de Rivoli, 1st; tel: 01 44 58 10 10; www.lemeurice hotel.com; Mon–Fri 7–10.30am, 12.30–2pm, 7.30–10pm, Sat–Sun 7–11am, 12.30–2pm, 7.30–10pm, closed Aug; metro: Tuileries; €€€€

The very best ingredients cooked in a subtle and understated way by chef Yannick Alléno. Some of the finest cooking in Paris.

Opéra and Grands Boulevards

Aux Lyonnais

32 rue St-Marc, 2nd; tel: 01 42 96 65 04; www.auxlyonnais.com; Tue–Fri noon–2pm, 7.30–10pm, Sat 7.30–10pm, closed Aug; metro: Grands Boulevards; €€€

Price guide for a two-course *à la carte* dinner for one with half a bottle of house wine:

€€€€	over 75 euros
€€€	50–75 euros
€€	30–50 euros
€	below 30 euros

Founded in 1892, this bistro still retains its original decor but has been beautifully revamped under top chef Alain Ducasse. The menu pays tribute to Lyonnaise specialities, with renditions of pike, perch and crayfish quenelles. Also highlights include frogs' legs, charcuterie, excellent cuts of beef and regional wines.

Chartier

7 rue du Faubourg Montmartre, 9th; tel: 01 47 70 86 29; daily noon–11.30pm; metro: Grands Boulevards; €

Chartier is the best-known low-price eatery in town. The atmosphere is an experience in itself, with Belle Epoque decor and snappy waiters, although there was some controversy a few years ago about the replacement of the checked tablecloths with white paper ones. Expect shared tables and plenty of bonhomie. Arrive early if you want to stand a chance of getting a seat.

Gallopin

40 rue Notre-Dame-des-Victoires, 2nd; tel: 01 42 36 45 38; www. brasseriegallopin.com; daily noon–midnight; metro: Bourse; €€–€€€

This brasserie opposite the Stock Exchange opened in 1876 and is still decorated in Belle Epoque style. The chef prepares refined versions of traditional dishes, including *pâté maison*, *steak tartare* and flambéed crêpes. The fish is a star attraction, with specialities such as haddock poached in milk with spinach, and delicious seafood platters. Excellent food in a distinguished setting.

Le Grand Colbert

2 rue Vivienne, 2nd; tel: 01 42 86 87 88; www.legrandcolbert.fr; daily noon–1am; metro: Bourse; €€€

This large, beautiful brasserie, which opened in 1830, offers the sort of traditional dishes that the French have always demanded from their brasseries. Choose from beef carpaccio, goat's cheese in pastry, sole meunière, Burgundian snails or frogs' legs in garlic, ripe cheeses, and creamy chocolate mousse and feathery light *îles flottantes* (soft meringues in custard).

Taillevent

15 rue Lamennais, 8th; tel: 01 44 95 15 01; www.taillevent.com; Mon–Fri L from 12.15pm, D from 7.15pm; metro: George V; €€€€

One of the most illustrious haute-cuisine restaurants in Paris, but still surprisingly unstuffy. The food is magnificent: the earthy signature, spelt, is cooked 'like risotto' with bone marrow, black truffle, whipped cream and parmesan and is truly heavenly. Jacket requested.

Beaubourg and Les Halles

Benoît

20 rue St-Martin, 4th; tel: 01 42 72 25 76; www.benoit-paris.com; noon–2pm, 7–10pm; metro: Hôtel de Ville, Chatelet; €€€€

At this vintage bistro, renowned for its excellent cooking and high prices, master chef Alain Ducasse offers timeless terrines and casseroles. Highly professional service. A very chic affair.

Above from far left: bright decor in St-Germain.

Free Bread
Bread is served free of charge with any meal, and you are entitled to as much as you can eat, so do not be afraid to ask for more.

Michelin Stars

These most revered of culinary stripes are taken extremely seriously in France. At time of printing, Paris had 14 restaurants with three stars (London, for example, had just two, and New York had six). Losing a star can mean a sharp decline in the number of a restaurant's customers as well as a dent in the chef's pride. In 2003, just the fear of dropping a star after a less-than-perfect score from a critic led chef Bernard Loiseau to commit suicide.

La Fresque

100 rue Rambuteau, 1st; tel: 01 42 33 17 56; daily noon–3pm, 7pm–midnight; metro: Les Halles; €–€€

Sitting elbow to elbow at one of the big wooden tables is part of the charm here, as is the decor (white faïence tiles, frescoes, etc). The bistro fare, such as beef stew and duck, is excellent, and the staff are friendly. Always one vegetarian main course.

Marais and Bastille

404

69 rue des Gravilliers, 3rd; tel: 01 42 74 57 81; Mon–Fri noon–2.30pm, 8pm–midnight, Sat–Sun noon–4pm, 8pm–midnight; metro: Arts et Métiers; €€

Packed, hip and atmospheric, with low seating and iron grilles on the windows casting lacy patterns through the dim interior on to the tables. The Moroccan menu features filo-pastry pies, lamb brochettes, an exotic selection of couscous and tagines, and fragrant Berber desserts. Respectably good food.

Auberge Pyrénées-Cévennes

106 rue de la Folie-Méricourt, 11th; tel: 01 43 57 33 78; Mon–Fri noon–2pm, 7–11pm, Sat 7–11pm; closed most of Aug and first week in Jan; metro: République; €€–€€€

There's a reason why this classy spot won a best bistro award recently: the waiters are friendly, the decor is unique (purple-and-white cloths, terracotta floors, and stuffed animal heads on the wall), and the hearty food is top-notch. Try lentil caviar or *frisée aux lardons* (salad with bacon), followed by cassoulet, pigs' feet, fish *quenelles*, and rum Babas or profiteroles.

Le Pamphlet

38 rue Debelleyme, 3rd; tel: 01 42 72 39 24; Tue–Fri noon–2.30pm, 7.30–11pm, Sat 7.30–11pm only, closed for two weeks in Aug and two weeks in Jan; metro: Filles du Calvaire; €€€

Most restaurants in this part of town are low-key local affairs, but chef Alain Carrère offers a more exciting French experience, and absolutely flawless quality. Squid-ink risotto with *escargot beignets* (snail fritters), and baked banana with spice-bread ice cream are just two examples on a menu that changes daily. The tables are nicely spaced out, and the decor is warmly provincial. Superb-value dinner menu at €35.

Champs-Élysées and Trocadéro

Alain Ducasse au Plaza Athénée

25 avenue Montaigne, 8th; tel: 01 53 67 65 00; www.alain-ducasse.com; Mon–Fri 7.45–10.15pm, Thur–Fri 12.45–2.15pm, closed last two weeks in Dec and mid-July to mid-Aug; metro: Alma-Marceau; €€€€

Price guide for a two-course *à la carte* dinner for one with half a bottle of house wine:

€€€€	over 75 euros
€€€	50–75 euros
€€	30–50 euros
€	below 30 euros

Cooking elevated to an art form from globetrotting chef Alain Ducasse, France's first recipient of six Michelin stars (three apiece for two restaurants), with the help of his acolyte Christophe Moret. According to Ducasse, his meals are not about fancy presentation but purity and essence of flavour. Expect truffles in abundance but also superb vegetables from Provence, where he first made his name. Jackets essential for men; tie recommended.

Guy Savoy

18 rue Troyon, 17th; tel: 01 43 80 40 61; www.guysavoy.com; Tue–Fri noon–2pm, 7–10.30pm, Sat 7–10.30pm; metro: Charles de Gaulle-Étoile; €€€€

It took some time for Savoy's imaginative haute cuisine finally to earn the highest Michelin rating. The son of a gardener, he has an obsession with vegetables that anticipated the current organics trend by more than a decade. Jacket required for men.

Pierre Gagnaire

Hôtel Balzac, 6 rue Balzac, 8th; tel: 01 58 36 12 50; www.pierre-gagnaire.com; daily noon–1.30pm, 7.30–9.30pm, closed one week in Apr and in Aug; metro: Charles de Gaulle-Étoile, George V; €€€€

Pierre Gagnaire is one of the most original and artistic chefs in the world, and the elaborate composition of his dishes verges on the Baroque: think suckling lamb rubbed in ewe's-milk curd and capers served with roasted rice, Chinese cabbage with toasted rice, and snails with fennel shoots. A visit to this sedate grey dining room is essential for intrepid gastronomes.

Le Pré Catelan

Route de Suresnes, Bois de Boulogne, 16th; tel: 01 44 14 41 14; Tue–Sat noon–1.45pm, 7.30–9.30pm, Sun noon–1.45pm, closed last week in Oct and three weeks in Feb; metro: Porte Maillot; €€€€

In the heart of the Bois de Boulogne, this is one of the most romantic spots in Paris. Frédéric Anton prepares spectacular haute cuisine centring on fresh truffles, lobster, lamb and fresh seafood. Reserve.

The East and Northeast

Le Chapeau Melon

92 rue Rebeval, 19th; tel: 01 42 02 68 60; daily, food served Wed–Sat eve only; metro: Pyrénées; €–€€

Olivier Camus's Belleville restaurant, the 'Bowler Hat' – a former wine shop – now does a simple, no-choice three-course set menu in the evenings with a fabulous wine list, including some excellent organic bottles (quite a speciality here). Charming and friendly local restaurant.

Le Square Trousseau

1 rue Antoine Vollon, 12th; tel: 01 43 43 06 00; www.squaretrousseau.com; daily 8am–2am; metro: Ledru-Rollin; €€–€€€

Inside this bistro is spacious, with Art Deco lamps, colourful tiles and burgundy velvet. There's also a heated terrace facing a leafy square. Gaz-

Le Fooding

A contraction of the words 'food' and 'feeling', this watchword of modern French cooking was invented by journalist Alexandre Cammas in 1999 as a creed for re-energising French cuisine. Among its central tenets are being open-minded, a desire for sincerity, fun and an appetite for innovation. Its attempt to blow away the old conservatism seems to have met with some success.

pacho, tuna tartare, rosemary lamb and spring vegetables, a superlative *steak tartare*, and raspberry gratin are among the delights available.

Le Train Bleu

1st floor, Gare de Lyon, 12th; tel: 01 43 43 09 06; www.le-train-bleu.com; daily 11.30am–3pm, 7–11pm; metro: Gare de Lyon; €€€

In the midst of the Gare de Lyon, the terminus for trains from the Mediterranean, this huge, impressive brasserie was built for the 1900 World Fair. With its frescoed ceilings depicting destinations served by the trains from the station, mosaics and gilt detailing, it is Second Empire style at its very grandest. Classic French dishes are well prepared and efficiently served. Good-value set menus.

Le Verre Volé

67 rue de Lancry, 10th; tel: 01 48 03 17 34; www.leverrevole.fr; closed Mon; metro: Jacques Bonsergent; €€

This wine shop-cum-restaurant close to the Canal St-Martin is cosy inside, with cheery green wooden chairs and dinky tables packed together. Wine bottles line the walls – you can choose from a small number by the glass or

else just pay a corkage charge on any of the 300 or so bottles for sale. The food is classic French fare.

Latin Quarter/St-Germain

Le Timbre

3 rue Sainte-Beuve, 6th; tel: 01 45 49 10 40; www.restaurantletimbre.com; Tue–Sat noon–2pm, 7.30–10.30pm; metro: Vavin, Notre-Dame-des-Champs; €€–€€€

Located near the Jardin du Luxembourg, in a vibrant, foodie-friendly area of the 6th dubbed the 'Quartier Vavin', British-born Christopher Wright's postage stamp-sized ('timbre' means stamp) eatery uses market-fresh produce to serve up French classics with an English twist. The well-executed set menu, costing around €30 per person and including service but not wine, has won rave reviews from critics in France and back across the Channel.

The 7th and 15th

L'Atelier de Joël Robuchon

5 rue de Montalembert, 7th; tel: 01 42 22 56 56; daily 11.30am–3.30pm, 6.30pm–midnight; metro: Rue du Bac, St-Germain-des-Prés; €€€

Even jaded Parisians queue up in all weathers to sample the warm *foie gras* brochettes or tapenade with fresh tuna conjured up by one of France's most revered chefs. The restaurant is built around an open kitchen, so you can watch the masters at work, and the atmosphere is slick, like that of a bar. Reservations are accepted for the sittings at 11.30am–12.30pm, 2–3.30pm and 6.30pm only.

Price guide for a two-course *à la carte* dinner for one with half a bottle of house wine:	
€€€€	over 75 euros
€€€	50–75 euros
€€	30–50 euros
€	below 30 euros

Le Florimond

19 avenue de la Motte-Picquet, 7th; tel: 01 45 55 40 38; Mon–Fri L and D, Sat D only, closed 1st and 3rd Sat of the month; metro: Ecole Militaire, Latour Maubourg; €€–€€€

Pascal Guillaumin's bistro has a cosy, intimate atmosphere. His traditional French dishes are beautifully presented, and the service is warm and friendly. There's a great-value three-course set menu at lunch time for around €20; the evening set menu is €35.

L'Os à Moelle

3 rue Vasco-de-Gama, 15th; tel: 01 45 57 27 27; Tue–Sat noon–2pm, 7–10.30pm, closed three weeks in Aug; metro: Lourmel; €€€

For high-quality food at a very reasonable price, this unpretentious corner bistro is a worthwhile destination. Chef Thierry Faucher prepares a different six-course, *prix-fixe* menu (around €40) every night, with two choices for each course. Don't worry about the limited menu: everything is very good and fabulous value for money. Cheerful, colourful, surprisingly simple decor, given the exceptional quality of the food.

Il Vino di Enrico Bernardo

13 boulevard de la Tour Maubourg, 7th; tel: 01 44 11 72 00; www.ilvino byenricobernardo.com; daily noon–2pm, 7pm–midnight; metro: Tour Maubourg, Invalides; €€€–€€€€

Milanese Enrico Bernardo turns the traditional dining tables upside down at his restaurant where the food plays second fiddle to the wine. Diners choose their wines and then learn what dishes are on offer to complement them – or else go the whole hog on a full blind-tasting menu. It seems gimmicky but it works.

Montparnasse and the New Left Bank

La Coupole

102 boulevard du Montparnasse, 14th; tel: 01 43 20 14 20; www.flobrasseries.com/coupoleparis; daily 8.30am–1am; metro: Vavin; €€€

This legendary Art Deco brasserie (the largest in Paris) opened its doors in 1927 and is still going strong. Now run by the Flo Brasserie group, it has a convivial atmosphere, and its popularity remains intact. The classic brasserie fare includes huge platters of shellfish, *choucroute* and Alsatian sausages, and steaks and hearty stews.

La Régalade

49 avenue Jean-Moulin, 14th; tel: 01 45 45 68 58; Mon 7–11pm, Tue–Fri noon–2pm, 7–11pm, closed Aug; metro: Alésia; €€

A destination bistro for epicures across Paris for over 10 years, La Régalade is now under new ownership. Chef Bruno Doucet has injected it with life, while retaining much of what was good about it, especially the reasonable pricing. Start with the complementary *pâté de campagne* with 'rustic' bread, then proceed with a cream of walnut soup poured over a flan of *foie gras*, duck hearts with oyster mushrooms, and Grand Marnier soufflé to finish. *Prix-fixe* menu is just over €30.

Above from far left: outdoor refreshment at place du Tertre in Montmartre; happy hour in St-Germain.

Vegetarians in France
The vegetarian dishes of French cuisine are few and far between, which can be trying for herbivorous travellers. Even dishes that you are assured are meat-free often contain bacon or meat-based stocks. A solution is to order two meat-free starters instead of a main course, or to stick to simple egg and potato dishes. In an up-market restaurant, you can telephone ahead and request a vegetarian meal; this gives the cook time to concoct something just for you. Another option is to explore the city's ethnic restaurants, which serve meat-free snacks as well as elaborate three-course meals.

Paris is legendary as a city of culture, with theatres, concert halls, cinemas, cabaret halls and clubs to suit every taste, housed in anything from an Art Deco palace or Japanese pagoda to a lighthouse or former Turkish baths. As would be expected of a major European capital, its theatres and music venues attract world-class performers in addition to serving as splendid showcases for the proliferation of home-grown talent. The following selection is just the tip of the iceberg.

Theatre

Comédie Française

1 place Colette, 1st; tel: 08 25 10 16 80 (from France)/033 1 44 58 15 15 (from outside France); www.comedie-francaise.fr; metro: Palais-Royal

Since 1799 France's national theatre, the Comédie Française, has performed at this fine neoclassical building by the Palais Royal. The majority of productions staged here are in the classical repertoire, by playwrights such as Corneille, Molière and Racine, although plays by more modern classic writers, including Genet and Anouilh, are also shown.

Odéon – Théâtre National de l'Europe

Place de l'Odéon, 5th; tel: 01 44 85 40 40; www.theatre-odeon.fr; metro: Odéon

First opened in 1782 as a venue for the Comédie Française *(see above)*, this grand neoclassical behemoth stages classics, translations of foreign works, and contemporary drama –

anything from Aeschylus to Heinrich von Kleist and Alexandre Dumas to new commissions.

Théâtre National de la Colline

15 rue Malte-Brun, 20th; tel: 01 44 62 52 52; www.colline.fr; metro: Gambetta

With two auditoria – one large, one small – this theatre puts on productions of French and international modern and contemporary drama, including works by Camus, Ibsen and Gerhart Hauptmann. Some productions are in the original language with subtitles.

Dance

Ballet de l'Opéra National de Paris

Bastille: 120 rue de Lyon, 12th; Palais-Garnier: Place de l'Opéra, 9th; tel: 08 92 89 90 90 (from within France)/+33 1 71 25 24 23 (from elsewhere); www.operadeparis.fr; metro: Bastille (for the Opéra Bastille) or Opéra (for the Palais-Garnier)

Classics and new productions are staged by the Ballet de l'Opéra under current dance director Brigitte Lefèvre. Most are shown in the sumptuous 19th-century Palais Garnier *(see p.44)*, although some are performed at the more modern Opéra Bastille *(see p.55)*.

Centre National de la Danse

1 rue Victor Hugo, Pantin; tel: 01 41 83 98 98; www.cnd.fr; metro: Hoche

The Parisian dance scene was given a lift in 2004 with the opening of this national centre to the northeast of the

city centre. The atmosphere is intimate, with performances in small studios.

Théâtre National du Chaillot

Palais du Chaillot, 1 place du Trocadéro, 16th; tel: 01 53 65 30 00;
www.theatre-chaillot.fr; metro:
Trocadéro

This Art Deco complex houses three auditoria (from small and intimate to a huge 2,800-seater), mostly used for global dance performances, although also some drama. There is also a bar with wonderful views of the Eiffel Tower.

Théâtre de la Ville

2 place du Châtelet, 4th; tel: 01 42
74 22 77; www.theatredelaville-
paris.com; metro: Châtelet

The city's leading contemporary dance venue, with a programme of national and international companies and productions. It works together with its sister venue, the Théâtre des Abbesses in Monmartre (31 rue des Abbesses, 18th; tel: as above; metro: Abbesses). Also stages theatrical productions and classical and world music concerts.

Music

Caveau de la Huchette

5 rue de la Huchette, 5th; tel: 01 43
26 65 05; www.caveaudela
huchette.fr; metro: St-Michel

Established in 1946, this jazz and swing club was frequented by GIs during World War II and has been going strong ever since, with big names such as Claude Bolling and Sacha Distel having performed here. Dancing continues into the small hours.

Opéra Nationale de Paris, Bastille and Palais-Garnier

For details, see p.122

The Opéra Bastille is the Opéra Nationale's main venue for operatic productions, with acclaimed young Swiss conductor Philippe Jordan the current Musical Director. Fans under 28 can enjoy cheap prices if they turn up on the day and there are still seats available.

Salle Cortot

78 rue Cardinet, 17th; tel: 01 47 63
85 72; metro: Malesherbes

Part of the Ecole Normale de Musique de Paris (the elite music school in France), this concert hall with exceptional acoustics (the French pianist Cortot, after whom it is named, claimed it 'sounds like a Stradivarius') puts on free student concerts.

Salle Gaveau

45 rue La Boétie, 8th; tel: 01 49 53
05 09; www.sallegaveau.com;
metro: Miromesnil

Gorgeous venue built in 1906–7 and the scene of legendary performances by Casals, Cortot and other musical greats. Piano recitals and chamber and orchestral music.

Salle Pleyel

252 rue du Faubourg-St-Honoré,
8th; tel: 01 42 56 13 13;
www.sallepleyel.fr; metro: Ternes

Built in 1927 by the piano makers after whom it is named, this concert hall with a fine Art Deco-style exterior is now home to the Orchestre de Paris, under Christoph Eschenbach. It mounts an

Above from far left: crowds gather at the Hôtel de Ville.

Paris Cinema International Film Festival
Every July Paris hosts its international film festival, with events taking place at 15 venues across the city. The festival incorporates an international competition, in which 12 feature films compete for several awards, as well as premieres of French film and special events such as outdoor screenings and even a flea market dedicated to cinema. Each year celebrates a different country's films. For more information, see www.pariscinema.org.

Above from left: musician outside the Louvre.

Clubs

Of Paris's many clubs, give the following a go: Les Bains Douches (7 rue du Bourg-l'Abbé, 3rd; tel: 01 53 01 40 60), a long-established club/restaurant/bar set in a former Turkish baths; Le Baron (6 avenue Marceau, 8th; no tel), a VIP nightclub where DJs and live bands provide entertainment; Batofar (11 quai François-Mauriac, 13th; tel: 01 53 60 17 30), a lighthouse ship on the Seine that offers an alternative night out; and Le Rex Club (5 boulevard Poissonnière, 2nd; tel: 01 42 36 10 96), a techno, house and drum 'n' bass stalwart, aimed more at hard-core clubbers than Parisian posers.

excellent international programme of orchestral concerts and recitals.

Théâtre des Champs-Elysées

15 avenue Montaigne, 8th; tel: 01 49 52 50 50; www.theatrechamps elysees.fr; metro: Alma Marceau or Franklin D. Roosevelt

Notorious as the scene of the premiere of Stravinsky's *The Rite of Spring* in 1913, this beautiful Art Nouveau theatre now puts on a broad programme of opera, classical music, jazz and world music concerts and dance.

Film

Le Balzac

1 rue Balzac, 8th; tel: 01 45 61 10 60; www.cinemabalzac.com; metro: George V

This stylish retro cinema shows the latest films, some of which are preceded by a short speech by the manager, as well as older films by season (silent movies, etc). Also hosts concerts.

Cinémathèque Française

51 rue de Bercy, 12th; tel: 01 71 19 33 33; www.cinematheque francaise.com; metro: Bercy

The headquarters of French cinema are based on the north side of the Parc de Bercy, in a building designed by Frank Gehry. The Cinémathèque has a repertory cinema, a bookshop, restaurant, museum, research centre and archive.

Forum des Images

Porte St-Eustache, Forum des Halles, 1st; tel: 01 44 76 63 00; www. forumdesimages.fr; metro: Les Halles

With five screens, the forum within Les Halles shows old films, usually in thematic seasons, and is also home to an archive of Paris on film. You can also watch items from the 6,500-item collection on the small screen.

La Pagode

57bis rue de Babylone, 7th; tel: 01 45 55 48 48; metro: St-François-Savier or Sèvres Babylone

Completely out of place in the otherwise smart, understated 7th *arrondissement*, this extraordinary 19th-century copy of a Japanese pagoda is now an arthouse cinema. Lavish interior and pretty, if overgrown, garden.

Cabarets

Le Lido

116bis avenue des Champs-Élysées, 8th; tel: 01 40 76 56 10; www.lido.fr; metro: George V, Franklin D. Roosevelt

The famous 'Bluebell Girls' high-kick their way through the Lido's spectacular shows with countless costume changes, 23 sets and myriad special effects. Probably the grandest of the cabaret shows.

Moulin Rouge

82 boulevard de Clichy, 18th; tel: 01 53 09 82 82; www.moulinrouge.fr; metro: Blanche

Marvel at the 'Doriss' dancers as they parade to perfection in magnificent costumes dripping with feathers, sequins and rhinestones. You don't get much change from 100 euros (prices start at around 80 euros for the show only) but it's crazily over the top and fun.

CREDITS

Insight Step by Step Paris
Written by: Michael Macaroon
Series Editor: Carine Tracanelli
Cartography Editor: James Macdonald
Picture Manager: Steven Lawrence
Art Editors: Ian Spick and Richard Cooke
Photography by: Apa: Kevin Cummins, Pete Bennett, Jerry Dennis, Annabel Elston, Britta Jaschinski, Michael Macaroon, Ilpo Musto and Clare Peel except: The Bridgeman Art Library 20T, 96TR; Photolibrary 89T; Corbis 21CT; Getty/Francisco Hidalgo 2/3; Musée Association Les Amis d'Edith Piaf 74BL; Musée de la Ville de Paris 53B; Paris Tourist Office/Fabian Charaffi 43TR; Topham Picturepoint 94CL; Flickr Gabyu 70T, Paris By Mouth 14TL, J Lastra 15BR, Oh Darling 40T, CGO2 78/79T, Jean-Louis Zimmermann 80TL; Wikipedia Frank chulenburg 88T, Hyancinthe Rigaud 91CR, Nadar 97BL; Disneyland Paris 98/99 (all)
Front Cover: main image: 4Corners Images; other images: iStockphoto
Printed by: CTPS-China

DISTRIBUTION

Worldwide
APA Publications GmbH & Co. Verlag KG (Singapore branch)
7030 Ang Mo Kio Ave 5
08-65 Northstar @ AMK, Singapore 569880
Email: apasin@singnet.com.sg

UK and Ireland
Dorling Kindersley Ltd (a Penguin Company)
80 Strand, London, WC2R 0RL, UK
Email: customerservice@dk.com

US
Ingram Publisher Services
One Ingram Blvd, PO Box 3006
La Vergne, TN 37086-1986
Email: customer.service@ingrampublisher services.com

Australia
Universal Publishers
PO Box 307
St. Leonards NSW 1590
Email: sales@universalpublishers.com.au

New Zealand
Brown Knows Publications
11 Artesia Close, Shamrock Park
Auckland, New Zealand 2016
Email: sales@brownknows.co.nz

CONTACTING THE EDITORS

We would appreciate it if readers would alert us to errors or outdated information by writing to us at insight@apaguide.co.uk or Apa Publications, PO Box 7910, London SE1 1WE, UK.

www.insightguides.com

INDEX

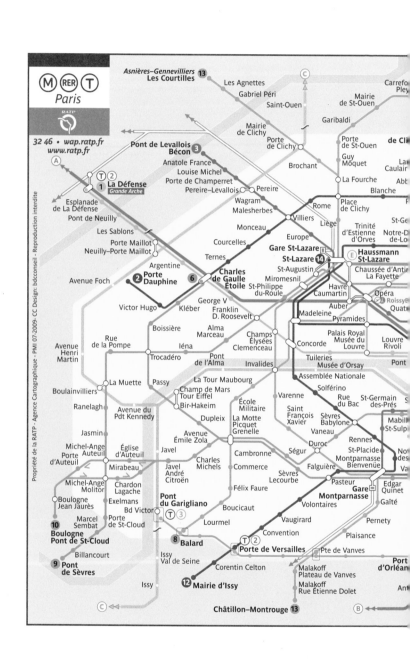